JOHN
RUSSWURM

JOHN RUSSWURM

Janice Borzendowski

Senior Consulting Editor
Nathan Irvin Huggins
Director
W.E.B. Du Bois Institute for Afro-American Research
Harvard University

CHELSEA HOUSE PUBLISHERS
New York   Philadelphia

Chelsea House Publishers

Editor-in-Chief Nancy Toff
Executive Editor Remmel T. Nunn
Managing Editor Karyn Gullen Browne
Copy Chief Juliann Barbato
Picture Editor Adrian G. Allen
Art Director Maria Epes
Manufacturing Manager Gerald Levine

Black Americans of Achievement

Senior Editor Richard Rennert

Staff for JOHN RUSSWURM

Associate Editor Perry King
Deputy Copy Chief Ellen Scordato
Editorial Assistant Jennifer Trachtenberg
Picture Researcher Amla Sanghi
Assistant Art Director Laurie Jewell
Designer Ghila Krajzman
Production Coordinator Joseph Romano
Cover Illustration Richard Daskam

First Printing

1 3 5 7 9 8 6 4 2

Library of Congress Cataloging-in-Publication Data

Borzendowski, Janice.
  John Russwurm.

  (Black Americans of achievement)
  Bibliography: p.
  Includes index.
  Summary: Traces the life and achievements of the early
spokesman against slavery who expressed his antislavery views
in *Freedom's Journal*, the first American newspaper owned and
operated by blacks.
  1. Russwurm, John Brown, 1799–1851—Juvenile literature.
2. Abolitionists—United States—Biography—Juvenile literature. 3. Afro-Americans—Biography—Juvenile literature.
4. Afro-Americans—Colonization—Liberia—History—19th
century—Juvenile literature. 5. Liberia—History—To
1847—Juvenile literature. 6. Journalists—United States—
Biography. [1. Russwurm, John Brown, 1799–1851. 2. Abolitionists. 3. Journalists. 4. Afro-Americans—Biography]
I. Huggins, Nathan Irvin, 1927–   . II. Title. III. Series.
E448.R96B67 1989   973'.0496073024 [B] 88-34082
ISBN 0-55546-610-9
     0-7910-0228-4 (pbk.)

CONTENTS

———— •❦• ————

On Achievement   7
Coretta Scott King

1
The Flames of Controversy   11

2
Of Two Worlds   17

3
College Life   33

4
The Power of the Press   41

5
A Change of Heart   55

6
Liberty's Shadow   67

7
Governor of a Free People   81

8
The Love of Liberty   95

Chronology   107

Further Reading   108

Index   109

BLACK
AMERICANS
OF
ACHIEVEMENT

MUHAMMAD ALI
heavyweight champion

RICHARD ALLEN
*founder of the
African Methodist
Episcopal church*

LOUIS ARMSTRONG
musician

JAMES BALDWIN
author

BENJAMIN BANNEKER
*scientist and
mathematician*

MARY MCLEOD BETHUNE
educator

BLANCHE K. BRUCE
politician

RALPH BUNCHE
diplomat

GEORGE WASHINGTON CARVER
botanist

CHARLES WADDELL CHESTNUTT
author

PAUL CUFFE
abolitionist

FREDERICK DOUGLASS
abolitionist editor

CHARLES R. DREW
physician

W. E. B. DUBOIS
educator and author

PAUL LAURENCE DUNBAR
poet

DUKE ELLINGTON
bandleader and composer

RALPH ELLISON
author

ELLA FITZGERALD
singer

MARCUS GARVEY
black-nationalist leader

PRINCE HALL
social reformer

WILLIAM HASTIE
educator and politician

MATTHEW HENSON
explorer

CHESTER HIMES
author

BILLIE HOLIDAY
singer

JOHN HOPE
educator

LENA HORNE
entertainer

LANGSTON HUGHES
poet

JAMES WELDON JOHNSON
author

SCOTT JOPLIN
composer

MARTIN LUTHER KING, JR.
civil rights leader

JOE LOUIS
heavyweight champion

MALCOLM X
militant black leader

THURGOOD MARSHALL
Supreme Court justice

ELIJAH MUHAMMAD
religious leader

JESSE OWENS
champion athlete

GORDON PARKS
photographer

SIDNEY POITIER
actor

ADAM CLAYTON POWELL, JR.
political leader

A. PHILIP RANDOLPH
labor leader

PAUL ROBESON
singer and actor

JACKIE ROBINSON
baseball great

JOHN RUSSWURM
publisher

SOJOURNER TRUTH
antislavery activist

HARRIET TUBMAN
antislavery activist

NAT TURNER
slave revolt leader

DENMARK VESEY
slave revolt leader

MADAME C. J. WALKER
entrepreneur

BOOKER T. WASHINGTON
educator

WALTER WHITE
political activist

RICHARD WRIGHT
author

ON ACHIEVEMENT

Coretta Scott King

BEFORE YOU BEGIN this book, I hope you will ask yourself what the word *excellence* means to you. I think that it's a question we should all ask and keep asking as we grow older and change. Because the truest answer to it should never change. When you think of excellence, perhaps you think of success at work; or of becoming wealthy; or meeting the right person, getting married, and having a good family life.

Those important goals are worth striving for, but there is a better way to look at excellence. As Martin Luther King, Jr., said in one of his last sermons, "I want you to be first in love. I want you to be first in moral excellence. I want you to be first in generosity. If you want to be important, wonderful. If you want to be great, wonderful. But recognize that he who is greatest among you shall be your servant."

My husband, Martin Luther King, Jr., knew that the true meaning of achievement is service. When I met him, in 1952, he was already ordained as a Baptist preacher and was working toward a doctoral degree at Boston University. I was studying at the New England Conservatory and dreamed of accomplishments in music. We married a year later, and after I graduated the following year we moved to Montgomery, Alabama. We didn't know it then, but our notions of achievement were about to undergo a dramatic change.

You may have read or heard about what happened next. What began with the boycott of a local bus line grew into a national movement, and by the time he was assassinated in 1968 my husband had fashioned a black movement powerful enough to shatter forever the practice of racial segregation. What you may not have read about is where he got his method for resisting injustice without compromising his religious beliefs.

He adopted the strategy of nonviolence from a man of a different race, who lived in a distant country, and even practiced a different religion. The man was Mahatma Gandhi, the great leader of India, who devoted his life to serving humanity in the spirit of love and nonviolence. It was in these principles that Martin discovered his method for social reform. More than anything else, those two principles were the key to his achievements.

This book is about black Americans who served society through the excellence of their achievements. It forms a part of the rich history of black men and women in America—a history of stunning accomplishments in every field of human endeavor, from literature and art to science, industry, education, diplomacy, athletics, jurisprudence, even polar exploration.

Not all of the people in this history had the same ideals, but I think you will find something that all of them have in common. Like Martin Luther King, Jr., they all decided to become "drum majors" and serve humanity. In that principle—whether it was expressed in books, inventions, or song—they found something outside themselves to use as a goal and a guide. Something that showed them a way to serve others, instead of living only for themselves.

Reading the stories of these courageous men and women not only helps us discover the principles that we will use to guide our own lives but also teaches us about our black heritage and about America itself. It is crucial for us to know the heroes and heroines of our history and to realize that the price we paid in our struggle for equality in America was dear. But we must also understand that we have gotten as far as we have partly because America's democratic system and ideals made it possible.

We are still struggling with racism and prejudice. But the great men and women in this series are a tribute to the spirit of our democratic ideals and the system in which they have flourished. And that makes their stories special and worth knowing. ❧

JOHN
RUSSWURM

———— ❦ ————

1

THE FLAMES
OF CONTROVERSY

A CRY OF "Traitor!" echoed through the streets of New York City.

One night in 1829, an angry mob of blacks gathered outside their ramshackle houses to pelt a crudely made, rag-stuffed dummy with stones, balls of mud, and pieces of garbage. The sign that hung around the dummy's neck bore the name of John Brown Russwurm, a black activist editor and one of the city's leading black citizens. On this night, however, his name drew nothing but curses and insults from the crowd, which cheered as a man stepped forward with a torch and set the ragged figure ablaze.

In a building not far from where the mob stood, Russwurm was busily preparing the next issue of *Freedom's Journal*, the first black newspaper in the United States. The commotion in the streets was nothing new to him: In the early 1800s, burning a person in effigy was a commonly used method for expressing violent disapproval of an individual's words or actions. New York's black residents were an especially hard-nosed group that included many runaway slaves, and Russwurm had often witnessed them holding

In 1829, a group of black New Yorkers burned an effigy of Russwurm on a city street after he announced his support of the American Colonization Society's efforts to settle former slaves in Africa. Five Points (shown here), one of the city's most heavily populated black neighborhoods in the late 1820s, was a common site for such public displays of outrage.

FREEDOM'S JOURNAL.

"RIGHTEOUSNESS EXALTETH A NATION."

CORNISH & RUSSWURM,
Editors & Proprietors

NEW-YORK, FRIDAY, MARCH 23, 1827

[VOL. I. No. 2.

MEMOIRS OF CAPT. PAUL CUFFEE

At this time, being about twenty years of age, he thought himself sufficiently skilled to enter into business on his own account. He laid before his brother David, a plan for opening a commercial intercourse with the state of Connecticut. His brother was pleased with the prospect, they built an open boat and proceeded to sea. Here for the first time his brother found himself exposed to the perils of the ocean, and the hazard of a predatory warfare which was carried on by the Refugees....

To be Continued.

From the Christian Spectator.
PEOPLE OF COLOUR.

The many recent movements in behalf of the children of Africa, give strong indications that better times are approaching for that portion of the human family....

A FRAGMENT

In one of those delightful autumnal evenings, in the month of October, when the celestial heavens appear in all their splendor and magnificence....

FROM ZION'S HERALD

(To be Continued.)

When Freedom's Journal, America's first black newspaper, was initially published in March 1827, it sent a wave of excitement through the nation's black communities. The journal's coeditors, Russwurm and Samuel Cornish, promised it would be an unrelenting voice for blacks in their battle for freedom and equal rights.

noisy public meetings to protest the savage institution of slavery that kept so many of their friends and relations in bondage in the South.

But circumstances on this night were different. It was not southern slaveowners who were the target of the mob's wrath but Russwurm himself. He had often been viewed as a hero by the black community: He had been one of the first black Americans to earn a college degree and had cofounded *Freedom's Journal.* A leading voice in the black struggle for equality and freedom, the newspaper publicized the efforts of antislavery groups seeking to liberate the 2 million blacks enslaved in the South, and it also crusaded for the country's 300,000 free blacks, who were allowed almost none of the rights that whites enjoyed. Black Americans dreamed of living as a free people, and Russwurm worked at turning their dream into a reality.

One of Russwurm's essays in *Freedom's Journal* angered the black citizens of New York, however, and led to the fire-filled night in 1829. In that article, he said that whites would never grant true equality to blacks. "We consider it a mere waste of words," he wrote, "to talk of ever enjoying citizenship in this country." No longer willing to battle for a cause that seemed hopeless, he announced that he had decided to embrace the views of the controversial American Colonization Society, a group founded on the belief that the best way to achieve black freedom lay in resettling former slaves in Africa.

The colonization movement had been the subject of heated debates within the black community ever since it had been founded by a group of white clergymen and philanthropists in the early 1800s. Some

Although Russwurm fought valiantly against slavery and racism in American society, he eventually became convinced that blacks would have to look elsewhere for a land of liberty. In 1829, he startled his newspaper's readers by announcing that any discussion of winning equality for blacks in America was a "waste of words."

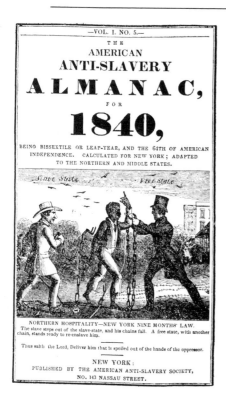

—VOL. I. NO. 5.—

THE
AMERICAN
ANTI-SLAVERY
ALMANAC,
FOR
1840,

BEING BISSEXTILE OR LEAP-YEAR, AND THE 64TH OF AMERICAN INDEPENDENCE. CALCULATED FOR NEW YORK; ADAPTED TO THE NORTHERN AND MIDDLE STATES.

NORTHERN HOSPITALITY—NEW YORK NINE MONTHS' LAW.
The slave steps out of the slave-state, and his chains fall. A free state, with another chain, stands ready to re-enslave him.

Thus saith the Lord, Deliver him that is spoiled out of the hands of the oppressor.

NEW YORK;
PUBLISHED BY THE AMERICAN ANTI-SLAVERY SOCIETY,
NO. 143 NASSAU STREET.

Antislavery journals called Russwurm a traitor for supporting the colonization movement, which many blacks saw as an attempt by whites to expel them from the land of their birth. One group of black New Yorkers proclaimed, "This is our home. . . . This is our country. . . . Here we were born, here we will die."

black leaders argued that the American Colonization Society's plans offered blacks a way to escape from tyranny and build a new home in Africa. The majority of blacks opposed the resettlement movement, however; they viewed it instead as a scheme by whites to rid the country of free blacks and thus weaken the struggle against slavery. By 1829, anticolonization sentiments in the black community had become so fierce that few antislavery leaders were even willing to discuss the issue.

For years, Russwurm himself had been a firm opponent of the colonization movement. He had believed that the efforts of antislavery crusaders such as himself would lead to an era of freedom for blacks. But slavery had continued to strengthen its iron grip over the South, and blacks who were fortunate enough to be free still remained trapped in a web of demeaning discriminatory laws. Gradually, he lost hope that whites would accept blacks as equals or let them live as a free people.

Russwurm believed that another option had to be considered, and the idea of black emigration to Africa began to seem increasingly attractive to him. Renouncing his newspaper's former opposition to African colonization, he braved the anger of his people when he declared:

> We have always said that when convinced of our error we would hasten to acknowledge it. That time has now arrived. The change which has taken place has not been the hasty conclusion of a moment; we have pondered much on this subject and read every article in our reach both for and against the [American Colonization] Society.

Reaction to Russwurm's announcement came quickly. The sense of betrayal that many blacks felt was summed up in the words of the noted white antislavery crusader William Lloyd Garrison. He wrote in his newspaper, the *Liberator*, "Russwurm's ingratitude is but too deeply stamped on the minds of many . . . which neither time nor space will ever obliterate."

Nevertheless, Russwurm remained convinced that he had found the best way for blacks to achieve the freedom they deserved. He bore the criticism of his friends and colleagues with great dignity. Even as he listened to people calling him a traitor, he knew in his heart that no one was more devoted than he to fighting for the liberty of black Americans.

Russwurm's unpopular stand on the African colonization issue cost him his high reputation in the black community. But it also led him to the cause to which he would devote the rest of his life. When the public outcry against him became too extreme for him to remain as editor of *Freedom's Journal*, he resigned from the newspaper and turned his energies to finding a place that would recognize blacks as equal citizens. A short time later, he accepted the American Colonization Society's offer of a post in its newly founded African colony of Liberia. The black colonists who had emigrated to Liberia were having a difficult time adjusting to their new home, and Russwurm believed he could improve the situation there.

In the fall of 1829, Russwurm put the bitter words of his critics behind him and began his journey by ship to a land named optimistically for liberty. He was inspired by a powerful vision of black freedom, and the opportunity to establish a protective haven for black Americans in Africa was a goal that seemed worth any sacrifice. Turning his eyes from the shores of America to the wide expanse of the ocean ahead of him, he was determined to prove that the struggle for black equality could be fought in many ways and in many places. **《》**

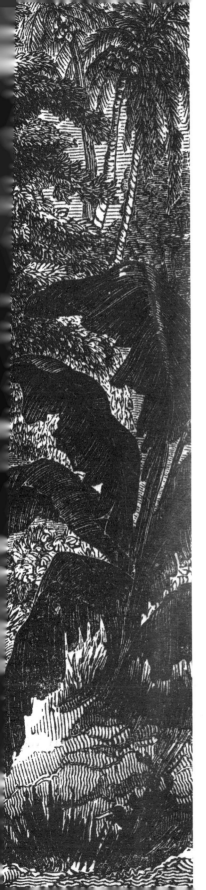

2
OF TWO WORLDS

❧

JOHN BROWN RUSSWURM was born in Port Antonio, Jamaica, on October 1, 1799. He was the son of a white American plantation owner and a black woman, and from the beginning of his life, his mixed racial heritage and light brown skin were birthrights that became sources of both fortune and conflict for him.

Because John had mixed blood, it was a stroke of luck for him to be born on an island in the British West Indies rather than in the United States. At the turn of the 19th century, it was rare for a slaveowner in America to admit he had fathered a mulatto (a person of mixed black and white ancestry). In fact, it was considered "gentlemanly" for a white man to be silent, even dishonest, about having sexual relations with a black woman.

In the British colony of Jamaica, however, there was much less prejudice against mulattoes. John's father, John Russwurm, Sr., was a prosperous planter who served his community as a judge, and he openly claimed to have sired the son of his black mistress. Accordingly, John's first years were spent on the Russwurm sugar plantation in relative comfort.

Nothing is known of John's mother, not even her name. She is never mentioned in the few remaining family letters and documents, and it is possible that she died in childbirth. Nevertheless, the racial legacy

Russwurm was born on a Jamaican sugar farm much like the one shown here. The only son of the plantation's white owner and his black mistress, he grew up in privileged circumstances.

he inherited from her would last a lifetime, and it instilled in him the motivation for his education, beliefs, and decisions. He spent his childhood and early adulthood among whites, but he would always regard himself as a black man.

The two worlds to which John belonged arose out of the cruel institution of slavery that was then practiced in almost every country in North and South America. Black slaves arrived in the Americas in 1511, less than two decades after Christopher Columbus made his first voyage to the New World and paved the way for European colonization. Faced with a need for workers to develop the New World's tremendous resources, European nations turned to Africa for a cheap and plentiful labor supply. Millions of Africans were kidnapped from their homes, chained in crowded and filthy slave ships, and transported on a long, deadly journey across the Atlantic

Slavers come ashore at an outpost on the African coast to pick up their human cargo. More than 40 million Africans fell victim to the slave trade that began in the early 1500s, and half of them died during the sea voyage to markets in the New World.

Ocean. The captives who survived the voyage were sold in markets and forced to labor in fields and mines until their death.

Most of the slaves on the West Indian islands worked on sugar plantations. Rum, molasses, and other products made from sugar were in heavy demand throughout the world, and the European nations jealously guarded their prized colonies. But one of the greatest threats to the colonial rulers came from the slaves themselves, who made up the vast majority of the population on most of the islands. Slave revolts occurred frequently in the West Indies, and some rebels had been successful in winning their freedom. While John was growing up, he probably heard tales about the Maroons, a group of fierce rebel slaves that escaped to the mountains of central Jamaica and defeated all attempts by the British to force them back into slavery.

In 1804, the world was shaken by the news that rebel slaves on the West Indian island of Santo Domingo had established the republic of Haiti, the first black nation in the New World. The Haitians' startling victory over well-trained French and Spanish armies was an inspiration to blacks throughout the Americas. Toussaint L'Ouverture, Henri Christophe, Jean-Jacques Dessalines and the other leaders of the Haitians' 13-year battle for independence became symbols of hope to millions of slaves in other countries who dreamed of winning their own freedom.

When John was eight years old, his quiet life on his father's Jamaica estate ended. In 1807, he traveled to Quebec, Canada, with his father, who was looking for land to buy. His father believed that John would receive a better education in Canada than in Jamaica and enrolled his son in a Canadian boarding school. When John Russwurm, Sr., returned to Jamaica, John, Jr., was left among strangers in a new and totally unfamiliar world.

Canada's cold north wind was the least of the shocks John had to endure. For the first time in his life, he found the color of his skin to be an issue. Although slavery was illegal in Canada, blacks and mulattoes were not considered the social equals of whites. Even his own father seemed to feel embarrassed about John's mixed parentage; he had enrolled his son in school under the name John Brown. Six years were to pass before John was again allowed to use the name Russwurm.

John must have felt like an outsider in Canada, but he was at least shielded from the extreme racial prejudice that existed across the border in the United States. Canada, which was part of the British Empire, had abolished slavery in 1793. Canadians may not have regarded blacks and mulattoes as equals, yet they were sympathetic to the plight of black Americans and offered refuge to America's fugitive slaves. By

the early 1800s, Canada had become the final stop on the Underground Railroad, a secret network that helped many American slaves escape north to freedom.

John lived in Canada until he was 13, when his father decided to leave Jamaica for good. Rather than move to Quebec, John Russwurm, Sr., traveled to Maine (then still a district in Massachusetts; it achieved statehood in 1820) and settled in the harbor town of Portland. Shortly thereafter, John received

Slave rebellions were a common occurrence in the West Indies and the United States, although most revolts were brutally suppressed. Slaves on the island of Santo Domingo, however, astonished the world in 1804 when they drove out their French rulers and established the black republic of Haiti.

his first glimpse of the United States. He was summoned to his father's new home and enrolled in a good private boarding school nearby. The Maine Genealogical Society recorded John's introduction to Portland in this way:

> The elder John Russwurm when he came to Portland brought with him a young mulatto boy 13 years old, who was named John Brown. He did not conceal the relationship that existed between them. He was proud of this son. He introduced him into the best society in Portland where he was honored and respected. He attended the best schools and had all the privileges that other boys of the best of families enjoyed.

John must have been confused that his father publicly claimed him as a son and yet refused to give him the name of Russwurm. Gradually, the youth began to realize that he would never be completely welcome within white American society because of his skin color. John's father was willing, however, to buck convention and place his son in an all-white school—an unusual step that involved John directly in the quest for black equality.

Blacks had been seeking their civil rights ever since the first slaves had arrived in the American colonies nearly two centuries earlier. The battle was waged with open defiance and moral persuasion—

Russwurm attended a school in Canada for five years before his father settled permanently in Portland, Maine.

Richard Allen (shown here) and Absalom Jones were among the clergymen who spearheaded the movement for racial equality in the North. "If you love your children," they proclaimed, "if you love your country, if you love the God of love, clear your hands from slaves."

and the voice of a million oppressed slaves was beginning to rumble through the land. How could a country that prided itself on being a champion of liberty and justice allow a system as inhumane as slavery to exist within its borders? opponents of slavery asked. Many Americans preferred to ignore the question. Yet the issue of slavery could not be avoided. In fact, it was already beginning to tear the new nation apart.

By the time John moved to America, all of the states north of Maryland had passed laws that either freed their slaves outright or provided for their gradual emancipation. Communities of free blacks existed in all of the major northern cities, although many of those cities, including New York, still had large populations of slaves who were as yet ineligible for emancipation. To help speed the path to liberty, philanthropic organizations known as manumission societies purchased many slaves from their owners.

Being free did not mean being equal—even for blacks in northern cities. Black religious and fraternal organizations such as the African Methodist Episcopal Church, the Free African Society, and the Prince Hall Freemasons had to wage a constant uphill battle to win civil rights for blacks and disprove widely held doctrines that blacks were an inferior race. Free blacks were barred from voting in most states, and discriminatory hiring practices limited the majority of them to such low-paying positions as field hands, maids, dockworkers, and chimney sweepers. Barred from almost all schools, blacks had little chance for education until a handful of black primary schools were founded in the late 1700s and early 1800s by churches and manumission societies.

For blacks in the southern states, there was little prospect of gaining even the most basic of human rights. Cotton was king from Virginia to Mississippi, and the economy of the South was totally dependent on slave labor. Southerners defended slavery as a necessary and even morally correct institution, and they were determined that nothing should stop them from practicing slavery or spreading it into newly acquired territories west of the Mississippi River. Despite the passage in 1808 of a federal law banning the importation of slaves from abroad, shipments of West Indians and captive Africans were brought in by smugglers. The hunger for more land and more field hands consumed the South, and there seemed little hope that slaves would soon be able to escape the sting of the overseer's lash.

In the North, determined groups of abolitionists —people who believed that slavery was evil—worked to bring about freedom for all blacks. Abolitionist leaders such as James Forten and the Reverends Richard Allen, Absalom Jones, and Peter Williams spread the antislavery message by organizing lectures and meetings, by distributing publications, and by sending petitions to Congress calling for an end to human bondage. Abolitionist literature found an eager audience among southern slaves, helping to fan the fires of rebellion and to incite uprisings such as the one led by Gabriel Prosser in Virginia in 1800. The southern states felt so threatened by the abolitionist onslaught that they pressured the North to restrict the activities of the antislavery organizations.

The growth of the antislavery movement caused one free black man in New York to write, "The time is fast approaching when the iron hand of oppression must cease to tyrannize over injured innocence." Yet the majority of whites remained convinced that blacks were inferior and fit only for menial work, southern slave catchers were still allowed to roam through northern cities kidnapping fugitive slaves and free blacks, and black families continued to be torn apart in slave markets throughout the South. An absolute victory of abolitionist ideals remained a distant prospect.

It was against this background of racial oppression and the black struggle for freedom that John Brown Russwurm began his life in the United States. His move from Quebec to Portland occurred during a stormy period in the relations between Americans and Canadians. In 1812, the United States declared war on Great Britain—partly in response to British violations of American shipping rights but also because of popular enthusiasm for the plot by American "war hawks" to annex Canada.

American armies marched into Canada and burned the town of York (later renamed Toronto), but stiff resistance from British and Canadian troops turned back the invasion. The British retaliated by capturing and burning Washington, D.C. When hostilities between the two countries finally ended in 1815, Canada remained part of the British Empire.

The War of 1812 must have aroused conflicting loyalties in John and made it even more difficult for him to feel a part of his new home. In addition, as a young man who was wrestling with his racial identity, he could not have helped but feel a strong resentment about the way America treated its black population. Neither the black sailors who manned the guns of their country's warships at the Battle of Lake Erie nor the black riflemen who helped General

While locked in a grim struggle against slavery and oppression, blacks also fought for their country in the American Revolution and other wars. Black soldiers such as the one shown here at right helped General Andrew Jackson rout British forces at the Battle of New Orleans during the War of 1812.

Concealed inside cartloads of hay or empty barrels, thousands of fugitive slaves were transported to safety in Canada and the North by an abolitionist network known as the Underground Railroad.

Andrew Jackson rout a British army at the Battle of New Orleans received ribbons for their bravery. But "disloyal" blacks who dared to plot a slave rebellion were quickly awarded a bullet or a noose.

Two events in early 1813 helped anchor John to his new country. First, his father bought 75 acres of farmland in Back Cove, Maine, an area now known as Westbrook. Having established himself among the well-to-do planters in the area, the elder Russwurm decided to marry. On May 4, 1813, he wed Susanna Blanchard, a young widow with three children.

The marriage proved to be as significant for John as for his father. His stepmother took an instant liking to her husband's 14-year-old mulatto son and insisted that he be brought home from boarding school and welcomed as a full member of the Russwurm household. John finally had a name, a home, and a family. His only blood sibling—a half brother, Francis Edward—was born in 1814.

One year later, John's father died. Fortunately for John, his stepmother's love remained very much alive. James Blanchard, one of Susanna Russwurm's children from her first marriage, later said of his mother's affection for John, "I sometimes josh Mother about her black son and tell her I am jealous, that she thinks more of him than she does of her white sons."

In 1817, Susanna Russwurm married a paper mill owner named William Hawes. John remained with the extended family—which eventually included 14 Russwurm, Blanchard, and Hawes children—while he attended Hebron Academy, a college preparatory school in Maine that was operated by the Baptist church. The school was open to all qualified students regardless of race.

No records about Russwurm's stay at Hebron Academy have survived, but he is said to have done well in all his studies. Like other college preparatory schools, the academy taught a curriculum of English grammar, Latin, mathematics, philosophy, and science. When Russwurm graduated from the school in 1819, he was already one of the best-educated blacks in the United States.

Determined to live in an intellectual center and also to become more deeply involved in the black struggle for freedom, John moved to Boston. The city boasted the largest black population in New England and was a leading center of antislavery agitation. He took a job teaching black children at a school in the home of Primus Hall, a prominent black businessman.

During Russwurm's four years in Boston, America became embroiled in a number of issues that directly concerned the welfare of blacks. On one question, congressmen from the North and South agreed: No more slaves should be imported from Africa. In an attempt to halt the booming smuggling trade that arose after the importation of slaves was outlawed, Congress passed legislation offering a reward of $50 per slave to anyone reporting the crime.

Americans were bitterly divided, however, on the question of whether slavery should be allowed in the territories west of the Mississippi River. Southerners demanded that slavery be allowed to spread unrestricted into the western regions. The northern states insisted that slavery must be confined to its existing borders and that any new state admitted to the Union should be a "free state"—one in which slavery was outlawed. In February 1820, senators from the North and South patched up their differences and passed an act called the Missouri Compromise. As part of this

At the age of 20, Russwurm graduated from Hebron Academy and took a job as a teacher at a black school in Boston, Massachusetts, a city that was a well-known center of black activism.

agreement, slavery was banned in western areas that were north of Arkansas's northern border.

Neither the young schoolteacher in Boston named John Russwurm nor the dozens of antislavery groups scattered throughout the country found much to cheer about during the period when the Missouri Compromise was debated. Slavery was sweeping westward in the South, and free blacks in the North were being burned out of their homes by racist mobs and prohibited from settling in many areas of the western territories. The need for strong-willed black leaders who could speak up for their people's rights had never been more urgent.

To Russwurm, the key to black progress was education. Believing that he could be of greater service to his people if he obtained more schooling, he became determined to graduate from college, a feat that no other black American had yet accomplished. While continuing his work with young students in Boston, he began to search for a college that was liberal enough to accept a black man.

In 1824, Russwurm's family encouraged him to apply to Bowdoin College in Brunswick, Maine. The Hawes family's influence may have been the deciding factor in helping Russwurm gain admittance to the college. In September, he became the first black ever to enroll there. ✦

3
COLLEGE LIFE

❧

Y THE TIME Russwurm arrived in Brunswick
in September 1824, Bowdoin College had begun to
emerge as one of the best of the small liberal arts
colleges for men that dotted the New England coun-
tryside. Founded in 1794 by wealthy settlers who had
moved to this remote corner of the Northeast, Bowdoin provided an alternative to Harvard, Yale, and
other good schools attended by the sons of upper-
class families. The surrounding town of Brunswick,
with its many fine grammar and college preparatory
schools, also had a reputation for being committed
to education.

At the age of 25, Russwurm was the oldest student
in his class when he enrolled as a junior (the college
decided that he was academically qualified to skip his
freshman and sophomore years). He joined a student
body that included many men who went on to great
fame: the author Nathaniel Hawthorne, the poet
Henry Wadsworth Longfellow, and a future president
of the United States, Franklin Pierce. The Bowdoin
campus later became known as the site where some
of the most unforgettable words about slavery and
black life were written: In 1852, Harriet Beecher
Stowe, the wife of a Bowdoin professor, published
Uncle Tom's Cabin, a powerful indictment of slavery
that helped to spread the influence of the abolitionist
movement.

*In 1824, Russwurm became the first black to be admitted to Bow-
doin College, in Brunswick, Maine.*

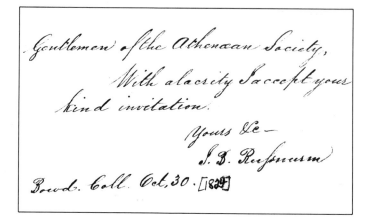

Two months after Russwurm began his classes at Bowdoin, he was invited to join the Athenaean Society, the college's literary fraternity. He accepted the invitation "with alacrity."

Russwurm found the atmosphere at Bowdoin to be intellectually stimulating, but the social life was not without its problems. Although Bowdoin records do not indicate any serious incidents of racism directed at its first black student, he was certainly treated differently from his white classmates. All the other students were required to rent rooms in the college's dormitories, but Russwurm boarded at a carpenter's home just outside of Brunswick. It is possible that he requested to live off campus so he could avoid racial confrontations, but it is more likely that the college asked him to seek separate housing.

Described by friends as humble, even shy, Russwurm was certainly one to avoid unnecessary conflict. He chose not to dwell on the injustice of his housing situation and instead focused on finishing his education. Having just gained a tenuous foothold in college, he knew he was not yet in a position to challenge the rules that governed the American educational system.

Russwurm became known to his teachers as a hardworking and dedicated student. He also succeeded in gaining the respect of his classmates. They recognized that black students who were given the opportunity to receive an education could perform as well as whites.

Russwurm's writing ability was noticed by Nathaniel Hawthorne, the president of the college's literary society. Known as the Athenaean Society, the organization was similar to a modern college fraternity. Hawthorne and another member of the society, Horatio Bridge, made a point of calling on Russwurm at his lodgings soon after he enrolled at Bowdoin. Hawthorne later sent a note to Russwurm, asking him to join the society. With a short reply—"Gentlemen of the Athenaean Society, with alacrity I accept your kind invitation"—Russwurm became the first black member of a college fraternity.

Extracurricular activities were only a small part of student life at Bowdoin. The students followed a

The only Bowdoin student to be housed off campus, Russwurm appreciated the effort made by Athenaean Society president Nathaniel Hawthorne to introduce him to activities at Bowdoin. Hawthorne later became one of America's best-known storytellers.

William Smyth, a mathematics and philosophy professor at Bowdoin, mixed political activities with his teaching duties. A leader of Brunswick's antislavery society, he helped broaden Russwurm's knowledge of the principles of the abolitionist movement.

strict schedule, and their curriculum was very different from the general studies found on almost any college campus today. The young men were expected to read *The Acts and Epistles of the New Testament* in Greek and to translate Cicero's *Select Orations* and Virgil's *Bucolics* from the Latin. They were also responsible for understanding the principles of philosophy and for mastering arithmetic and geography.

Students at Bowdoin arose at dawn. After attending chapel and spending one hour reciting from assigned readings, they had breakfast. Three hours of study followed the morning meal, and three more hours of study followed lunch. There were mandatory prayers before dinner, and all socializing had to be carried on between dinner and the time the lights were turned off in the early evening.

Like all students, Russwurm had favorite professors, and he especially admired William Smyth and Thomas Upham. Smyth, an assistant professor of mathematics and philosophy, was also a fierce abolitionist and helped establish an antislavery organization in Brunswick. Upham, a philosophy professor, was the same age as Russwurm. As a "conductor" on the Underground Railroad, he hid fugitive slaves who were trying to escape across the Canadian border, where no slave catchers could pursue them. Upham was also an early supporter of the American Colonization Society, and he may have been the person who first discussed with Russwurm the idea of resettling free black Americans in Africa.

During his senior year, Russwurm began to plan for his life following graduation. He intended to become a doctor, and he attended lectures in anatomy and chemistry to prepare himself for a career in medicine. His goal was to establish a medical practice in Haiti, the black nation in the West Indies that had won its independence from France more than two decades earlier. He wrote in a letter to a relative,

"After August, brighter prospects will dawn upon my efforts of many years. I am invited by the Haytian Government. I shall study medicine in Boston previous to an emigration to Hayti."

Russwurm had long been intrigued with Haiti, and he had written letters to the country's leaders. During his time at Bowdoin, his commitment to black equality had gradually become the overwhelming force in his life, and his interest in Haiti stemmed from his desire to live in a country free of slavery and racial oppression. He was thrilled, therefore, when the Haitian government invited him to settle there.

When Russwurm graduated from Bowdoin on September 6, 1826, he won the distinction of being

The revolutionary spirit of the Haitian liberator Toussaint L'Ouverture ultimately had a powerful effect on Russwurm. While at Bowdoin, he made plans to study medicine and settle in Haiti.

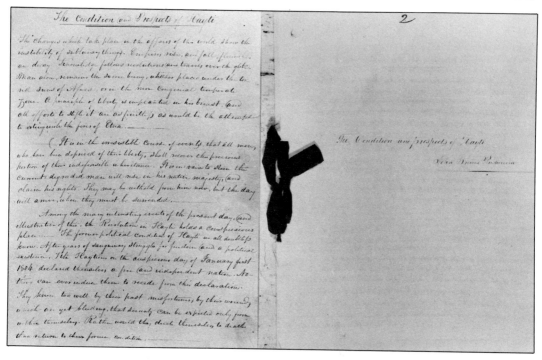

Russwurm used the Haitian revolution as the theme of his commencement address at the Bowdoin graduation ceremony in 1826. He said of every black man, "A principle of liberty is implanted within his breast, and all efforts to stifle it are as fruitful as the attempt to extinguish the fires of Etna."

the second black man to earn a college degree in America: Two weeks earlier, a black student named Edward Jones had graduated from Amherst College in Massachusetts. The *Eastern Argus*, a Portland, Maine, newspaper, joined in the congratulations to Russwurm, writing that he "has conducted himself with great propriety during the whole course of his college life, and has always enjoyed the esteem of his classmates." His high academic performance prompted Bowdoin to select him as one of the speakers at the graduation ceremony.

Russwurm felt deeply honored that he had been asked to speak at the commencement. But he was also nervous. The *Eastern Argus* described the historic moment when a black student first spoke at the graduation ceremonies of an American college: "Mr. Russwurm, a person of African descent, came on the stage under an evident feeling of embarrassment, but finding the sympathies of the audience in his favor, he recovered his courage as he proceeded."

Russwurm's speech, which he called "The Condition and Prospects of Hayti," touched on his plans to settle on the West Indian island and on his dreams for black equality. Referring to the great changes that had taken place in Haiti since the slaves had won their independence, he declared that the Haitians were "no longer the same people. . . . Haytians in slavery showed neither spirit not genius, but when Liberty, when once Freedom struck their astonished ears, they became new creatures: stepped forth as men, and showed to the world, that though Slavery may benumb, it cannot entirely destroy our faculties."

Russwurm's subject was a daring one to present to an all-white audience. Not all of his listeners were sympathetic to Haiti or to equal rights for blacks. Nevertheless, newspapers in Boston printed parts of his speech and stated that he had given the most important address at the commencement.

Shortly after the graduation ceremonies, Russwurm changed his mind about studying medicine and settling in Haiti. He decided instead to become involved in the crusade against slavery. Working for the abolitionist movement in America, it seems, turned out to be more important to him than living in a nation where slavery was already outlawed. So, in the fall of 1826, he moved to New York City, where the cry for freedom was being raised with a new power and a new urgency. ◗

4
THE POWER
OF THE PRESS

NEW YORK BOASTED the second largest free black population in America (Baltimore, Maryland, had the largest) when Russwurm arrived there in the fall of 1826. The city's black community had formed its own churches, social organizations, schools, and self-improvement societies, and it also had its own theater. Russwurm was delighted to find that the city also had an active group of educated middle-class blacks who were committed to attacking the evils of slavery and racial discrimination.

But despite these signs of progress, black New Yorkers were as miserably treated as the free blacks in other American cities. For most of them, life involved a constant battle against disease and hunger. Many were forced by poverty to live in a filthy, crowded neighborhood known as Five Corners (located in an area that is now called the Lower East Side), which was reputed to be the most crime-ridden slum in America. Black laborers who attempted to find jobs as skilled tradesmen were often violently handled by white workers, and the flood of thousands of unskilled Irish immigrants into the city made even menial jobs hard to find.

New York was a rapidly growing city when Russwurm arrived there in 1826. Although he was appalled by the racist articles printed in some New York newspapers, he was pleased to find that the city was home to many educated and politically aware black community leaders.

Although the majority of blacks in New York were free, slavery still cast an ugly shadow over life in the city. A sizable number of slaves still labored there, and many fugitive slaves from the South had settled in the city as well. Those who thought New York was a safe refuge were mistaken, for it contained thugs known as Blackbirders, who kidnapped fugitives and free blacks alike and then smuggled them out of the city to slave markets in the South.

By 1826, a growing number of blacks had decided it was time to step forward and challenge the oppressive conditions under which they and other blacks were forced to live. Black clergymen, including longtime community leader Peter Williams and the militant abolitionist Samuel Cornish, played prominent roles in rousing the black community. In 1826, Cornish issued an influential letter that he called *A Remonstrance Against the Abuse of Blacks*. Cornish's letter, which attacked racial injustice, was published in several newspapers and was widely discussed in the black communities of many cities.

Spurred on by an increasing feeling of desperation, black New Yorkers began to meet in churches and convention halls to discuss their grievances and to form plans to fight for their rights. Among the chief injustices they wanted corrected were the state laws that barred nearly all blacks from voting and that denied blacks the right to testify against whites in court.

The growing demand for equal rights by free blacks in northern cities did not go unopposed. Many whites, especially those whose livelihoods depended on their business connections with southern cotton growers, believed racial equality was a dangerous principle. These opponents of black progress made numerous statements about blacks that now seem preposterous but were widely believed at the time. Among other charges, the racists stated that blacks were happier as slaves than as free people.

When the first copies of Freedom's Journal were published on March 16, 1827, editors Samuel Cornish and John Russwurm told their patrons: "We wish to plead our cause. Too long have others spoken for us."

Among the most powerful tools of the racists' campaign against black equality was the press, which was entirely owned and operated by whites. Only a few northern newspapers showed any sympathy for black causes, and some actively campaigned to stir up ill feelings toward blacks. One New York editor, Mordecai Noah, who owned several newspapers, printed frequent attacks on blacks and attracted a circle of influential politicians and businessmen who joined him in opposing any reforms to aid the city's suffering black population.

New York's black leaders knew that a voice was needed to counter the racist propaganda of men such

The Reverend Samuel Cornish had already distinguished himself as a crusader for the rights of blacks when he was appointed chief editor of Freedom's Journal. *His connections with black leaders in New York and other cities helped the newspaper gain a solid footing in black communities around the country.*

as Noah. Although the black community had white sympathizers, they were generally reluctant to publicly support black demands for emancipation and equal rights. To make progress in the battle against racial oppression, however, blacks needed to speak for themselves and to reach out to all people who were friends of freedom.

Early in 1827, a group of black men—Russwurm among them—met in New York City to establish their own newspaper. They had witnessed the power of the press when it was directed against them, and now they decided it was time to use the press to their advantage. The founders of *Freedom's Journal*—the first newspaper in the United States to be owned and published by blacks—stated that the time had come "when the lies of our enemies should be refuted by forcible arguments. Daily slandered, we think that there ought to be some channel of communion between us and the public, through which a single voice may be heard, in defense of five hundred thousand free people of color."

The founders of *Freedom's Journal* appointed Samuel Cornish to be the chief editor of the newspaper. Apparently, Russwurm's abilities as a writer must have already made a strong impression on his new acquaintances in New York, for he was selected to share the editorial duties with Cornish. Cornish was four years older than Russwurm and had also been born free. Raised in Philadelphia and New York, Cornish was a graduate of the African Free Schools, a system of education for blacks begun in New York in 1787, and had founded New York's Negro Presbyterian Church.

The first edition of the weekly newspaper came off the printing press on March 16, 1827—only six months after Russwurm's college graduation. Black communities throughout the country immediately congratulated the two editors. By establishing and supporting a black newspaper in the face of overwhelming resistance, *Freedom's Journal's* founders were taking a major step toward uniting their people in the cause of liberty and giving them hope that a new era of progress for blacks was beginning.

The "voice of the colored people of America," as *Freedom's Journal* came to be known, had two major goals. Its first aim was to discredit the idea that blacks were inferior to whites, thus opening the way to racial equality. The newspaper also campaigned for the abolition of slavery throughout the country.

Cornish and Russwurm were determined to restore dignity to the black community. Black pride had been severely weakened by slavery and oppression. The young editors spent many hours combing through historical works looking for information about famous and successful blacks. Although the contributions of blacks were omitted from most historical writings, Russwurm and Cornish found mention of a few successful blacks.

The first edition of *Freedom's Journal* introduced its readers to Paul Cuffe, the son of a former slave. Cuffe was born in 1759 to an Indian mother and a black father. Against tremendous odds, he earned enough money working as a sailor to buy a ship, which eventually became part of a small fleet of merchant vessels that he operated. His shipping business brought him great wealth and respect, and he used these assets to fight for racial equality, ultimately playing a prominent part in gaining voting rights for blacks in Massachusetts. He spent his final years helping free blacks who wanted to leave America to emigrate to the British colony of Sierra Leone in West Africa.

Cuffe's memoirs were printed as a continuing feature in *Freedom's Journal*, and readers anxiously awaited each new episode. By writing about Cuffe and other notable blacks such as the poet Phillis Wheatley and the scientist and mathematician Benjamin Banneker, Russwurm and Cornish hoped to

Shipowner Paul Cuffe was the first person to be featured in Freedom's Journal's *weekly column on black Americans of achievement. An ardent civil rights activist based in Massachusetts in the late 1700s, he spent the last years of his life organizing efforts to help blacks emigrate to Africa.*

Mathematician, astronomer, surveyor, social reformer, and publisher of an annual almanac, Benjamin Banneker was a man whose accomplishments clearly demonstrated Russwurm and Cornish's contention that blacks were the equals of whites in intelligence.

inspire pride and ambition in their readers. They wanted to prove to their readers that blacks were capable of great achievements and that it was possible for free blacks to succeed in America.

The editors took a direct and uncompromising stand on the issue of slavery. They called for immediate emancipation, with financial assistance for the freed slaves. The journal also launched a vigorous attack on the racist ideas about black inferiority, describing the black viewpoint with great dignity and intelligence. Russwurm and Cornish resisted the impulse to respond in the same vicious manner that was used to defame the black race. To one particularly hateful article printed about blacks, the journal's editors ended their response by saying of the author, "We will have [the] charity to believe him ignorant rather than dishonest, and ascribe it to that ignorance rather than a vicious motive."

Russwurm and Cornish also addressed newsworthy events and social issues that affected the black community. Each edition of the newspaper—which was 16 pages long, with 4 columns of type on each page—included a variety of articles (including biographical features such as the one on Cuffe), poems and essays by black writers, and reports on the condition of black schools. Occasionally, the journal took up a particular cause, as when it campaigned for the release of poet Gilbert Horton, who had been wrongfully imprisoned as a fugitive slave.

News stories in *Freedom's Journal* ranged from articles on foreign, domestic, and local issues to marriage announcements, obituaries, and court trials. The coverage of everyday events within the black community helped blacks to feel a new sense of importance about their lives. In an attempt to discredit the widely held notion that blacks had no cultural heritage and no interest in family life, the journal printed articles that reaffirmed the customs and traditions blacks had brought with them from Africa, concentrating especially on the necessity of preserving strong family ties. In addition, the paper stressed the importance of education for black children, advertising the African Free Schools and listing schools open to black children throughout the country.

Russwurm and Cornish's commitment to helping blacks gain greater educational opportunities extended beyond the pages of their journal. Russwurm was appointed secretary of the African Dorcas Association, a society organized to provide decent clothing for the children of poor families so that they would not have to go to school in rags. Cornish visited parents to encourage them to send their children to school regularly.

The plight of black women—who were doubly oppressed because of their sex as well as their color—was another topic that Cornish and Russwurm addressed in their journal. The editors praised black

Realizing that education was the key to black progress, Russwurm and Cornish published many articles urging their readers to make whatever financial sacrifices were necessary to send their children to school. This engraving of a New York African Free School is based on a 13-year-old student's drawing of his school building.

women for their courage under the difficult conditions of slavery and encouraged the coming of a "new woman." The newspaper published several articles by an anonymous black woman, who described the active part that her sisters could play in remaking society. The author, who used the pen name "Matilda," called for greater educational opportunities for all women so that their talents could be put to better use than learning "the various mysteries of pudding-making."

The editors of *Freedom's Journal* used their newspaper to celebrate every advance in the cause of black liberty. On July 4, 1827, less than four months after the journal was founded, black New Yorkers had good reason to exult: Most of the slaves in the state were emancipated on a day that became known within the black community as Freedom Day. Abolitionist groups and charity organizations immediately began efforts to help the newly freed slaves find employment and housing.

Freedom's Journal was a resounding success during its first half year. Besides writing and editing articles, Russwurm and Cornish found sales agents for their

An illustration from an 1839 abolitionist publication shows a white mob destroying a black school. Russwurm and other crusaders for black education battled severe racial prejudice in both the northern and southern states, many of which had passed laws making it a crime to teach blacks how to read and write.

newspaper throughout the northern states, in Canada, Haiti, and England, and even in some of the southern states. This distribution network helped to increase readership and encourage an international following for the newspaper.

Despite the growth of the newspaper's circulation figures, it was still plagued by financial difficulties. Funds gathered from subscriptions and advertisements never seemed to meet the newspaper's expenses. The three-dollar annual subscription price was a lot of money for poor black families, and the editors constantly had to prod readers to pay up their overdue accounts.

As Russwurm and Cornish saw it, supporting the nation's only black newspaper was just one part of the campaign to uplift and unite the black community. The editors called upon blacks to take responsibility for each other, especially for those still in bondage. They urged their readers to join antislavery

A mother is separated from her young child at a slave market. Freedom's Journal published many articles describing the horrors of the slave system, and it was the first American newspaper to report the lynching of a black man and call for the prosecution of his murderers.

groups and "to be fearless, but patient, and to meet your enemies with logic and wit, instead of hate."

Russwurm and Cornish also pressed ahead with their campaign to change white attitudes toward blacks. Stating that the journal's articles had proved that blacks were by nature equal to whites, the editors claimed that only the effects of slavery and racial discrimination kept blacks mired in poverty and ignorance. They asked, "Would not the whites, deprived of opportunity for education and denied the respect to their manhood, be as ignorant and degraded under the same circumstances?"

Perhaps the thorniest issue that *Freedom's Journal* dealt with was the debate over the African colonization movement. The idea of resettling free blacks in Africa had been discussed in the years before the American Revolution. The movement finally gained strong support in 1816, when a Presbyterian clergyman named Robert Finley founded the American Colonization Society. The group's original members—all of them white—included President James Madison, former president Thomas Jefferson, Senator Henry Clay, and other powerful politicians and businessmen. The goals of these men were summed up in Jefferson's statement, "Let the ocean divide the white man from the man of color."

To most black leaders, the motives of the society's founders were highly questionable. Although Finley and Jefferson seemed genuinely concerned about helping blacks escape from oppression in America, Clay summed up the viewpoint of the most hardened racists when he stated that colonization would "rid our country of a useless and pernicious, if not dangerous, portion of its population"—the free blacks. Nevertheless, the society's program attracted many free blacks who despaired of ever achieving equality and justice in America and who believed that the only path to true freedom was for them to return

Freedom's Journal fostered a growing feeling of independence and militancy among blacks. The newspaper devoted much of its space to reporting the activities of abolitionist groups and black organizations such as this African Methodist Episcopal Church congregation.

to Africa and form an independent, self-governing colony.

In 1819, the American Colonization Society was awarded a large grant of money by Congress to build a settlement on the west coast of Africa. Three years later, a group of black American settlers established the colony of Liberia. They called the capital Monrovia after President James Monroe, who had approved the federal funding for the expedition. On April 22, 1822, the American flag flew for the first time in the West African colony of Liberia.

By 1827, when *Freedom's Journal* began to publish articles disputing the policies of the American Colonization Society, the organization had built a stronghold in the United States. The society gained supporters among whites who believed that America would lose its racial and cultural identity if blacks were given equality and who viewed free blacks as instigators of slave uprisings and as unwanted competition for white laborers.

The debate over the colonization movement frequently broke down into bitter disputes among blacks and their white abolitionist allies. Some blacks welcomed the promise of freedom and equality in Africa. The majority, however, refused to leave America, believing themselves Americans, not Africans. Many had been born in the United States and knew nothing of the land of their parents or grandparents. They were furious that whites, already having kidnapped blacks from Africa, were now trying to push them out of their new homeland. In addition, many of them believed that the colonization plan was a scheme to drive black abolitionists out of the country and strengthen slavery's grip on blacks still in bondage.

President James Monroe helped the American Colonization Society gain federal funding for its program of settling freed slaves in Africa. In gratitude for the president's support, the organization chose the name Monrovia for the capital of its African colony, Liberia.

The feelings of the American Colonization Society's black opponents were summed up in 1817, at a convention organized by James Forten and Richard Allen in Philadelphia. The delegates at the meeting issued the following statement: "Whereas our ancestors (not of choice) were the first successful cultivators of the wilds of America, we their descendants feel ourselves entitled to participate in the blessings of her soil, which their blood and sweat manured."

Russwurm and Cornish were among the blacks who opposed the colonization movement. Yet they used *Freedom's Journal* to present all sides of the controversy. Although they urged their readers to discuss the issue and to make their own decisions, they made clear their belief that the best interests of blacks would not be served by the American Colonization Society. Cornish wrote, "Abide in the United States, or you can't be saved." Both men denounced the advocates of resettlement and stated firmly their own intention to stay in America.

Russwurm, Cornish, and *Freedom's Journal* played a vital role in the controversy over the colonization movement. Until the paper was established, there was no way for black leaders to express their doubts about the American Colonization Society except by word of mouth. The concerns of black leaders went unheeded until Russwurm and Cornish took up the cause and insisted on being heard. "We are in a land of Liberty," they wrote, "and though prejudices are against our acting as freedmen, they shall not compel us to relinquish our pens."

By August 1827, Russwurm and Cornish had successfully broken the white monopoly on the press. Finally, black voices were being heard in America. The two editors took pride in their partnership and accomplishments. Their future as leaders of America's black community seemed assured.

Then, one month later, everything changed. ❧

5

A CHANGE
OF HEART

◆

SIX MONTHS AFTER the first issue of *Freedom's Journal* was printed, the newspaper's readers were stunned to learn that Samuel Cornish and John Russwurm were ending their partnership. Cornish had decided to give up his position as editor. His letter of resignation, which appeared in the newspaper on September 14, 1827, stated: "Fully persuaded that it will be for my health and interest, I have resolved to remove to the country . . . to devote myself exclusively to the work of the ministry."

The breakup of the editorial team caused more than just a change in the management of the newspaper. Because Cornish did not move to the country or immediately devote himself to the ministry, rumors began to spread around the city that political differences with Russwurm had caused the split. The reports implied that Cornish had wanted to take a much firmer stance against the American Colonization Society than Russwurm was willing to take.

There were strong reasons for the rumors: Cornish's articles had displayed a far more radical viewpoint than Russwurm's. The two men's different political ideals were a natural result of the differences

Boston police disrupt an 1858 meeting of militant abolitionists. Russwurm refused to side with the more radical members of the antislavery movement who advocated the use of violence to win freedom for blacks.

FREEDOM'S JOURNAL.

"RIGHTEOUSNESS EXALTETH A NATION."

BY JNO. B. RUSSWURM.　　　　NEW-YORK, FRIDAY, MARCH 14, 1828.　　　　VOL. I.—NO. LI

in their backgrounds. Russwurm's close involvement with his white family made him less suspicious of the white population in general. Cornish, who had lived among blacks all his life, distrusted whites when it came to leading the battle for racial justice. He believed that only blacks could know what was best for their people.

Despite the rumors, Cornish's resignation was not due to bad feelings between the two editors. He maintained his ties with Russwurm and *Freedom's Journal* after his resignation, serving the newspaper as a sales agent. Cornish had simply decided to devote himself in other ways to the struggle for black rights. After leaving the journal, he campaigned for the abolitionist movement and for education for black children. Later, he started other publications, including a militant black journal called *The Colored American*.

Cornish's resignation was a major turning point in Russwurm's publishing career. Cornish enjoyed a great deal of influence with a group of black intellectuals in New York, and many of these men believed that *Freedom's Journal* suffered a sharp drop in the quality of its journalism as soon as Russwurm became the paper's sole editor. These critics complained that the stories now lacked originality, compromised on issues, and were often vague and pointless.

Letters of protest piled up on Russwurm's desk, many of them charging that the newspaper was not giving enough attention to newsworthy events that directly affected the black community. The complaints were at least partly justified. At times, Russwurm filled the pages with literary pieces, leaving out

BY JNO. B. RUSSWURM. NEW-YORK, FRIDAY, MARCH 14, 1828. VOL. I.—NO. LI.

THE COLORED AMERICAN.

SAMUEL E. CORNISH, Editor.

New-York, Saturday, May 13, 1837.

PHILIP A. BELL, Proprietor.

the news altogether or giving it only a few lines of space. In one issue, published a month after Cornish resigned, Russwurm covered the entire front page with a reprint of a literary essay that had previously been printed in the newspaper.

Russwurm generally ignored his critics. But in December 1828, three months after taking over as senior editor, he angrily wrote: "Our course has always been an independent one. . . . In literature, as in politics, we wish for no king, no dictator." He never admitted that the journal lacked focus or was suffering any shortcomings in quality. On one occasion, however, he agreed that the appearance of the paper had become sloppy. After he was told that pages had been placed out of order and many words had been left out of an issue, he printed an apologetic notice that stated, "There were novices in the print shop."

Many of the newspaper's subscribers were patient with Russwurm. They realized how difficult it was to run the newspaper single-handedly and were willing to give him time to adjust to his increased responsibilities. For every detractor, he had many supporters who echoed the sentiment of one black activist, who said of Russwurm, "There are few men who have lived whose editorial pen could battle with such force against a volcano of sin and oppression." But the words of the newspaper's critics, coupled with growing unrest between blacks and whites, eventually began to discourage Russwurm.

Although Russwurm was happy about the sense of racial pride that *Freedom's Journal* had aroused in

When Samuel Cornish resigned from Freedom's Journal *in September 1827, it was speculated that he and Russwurm had quarreled about politics. After the split, Cornish worked for the abolitionist movement and published a militant black journal,* The Colored American.

its readers, it troubled him to think that white bigots might be using his articles to instigate attacks on black communities. In a number of cities in the North, black neighborhoods were being destroyed by rampaging white mobs, and campaigns had begun to drive blacks completely out of some towns. Racial tensions seemed to be getting worse instead of better.

Blacks fought back against the attempts to intimidate them. In New York and other cities, they organized self-protection groups known as vigilance committees to guard against white attacks and to assist fugitive slaves. The idea of holding conventions of black groups from around the nation also began to take hold around this time.

The rise of black militancy did not make Russwurm's job any easier. Since the founding of *Freedom's Journal* had established him as a spokesman for his people, he had been under heavy pressure. Every word he printed in the newspaper was scrutinized closely, and different groups called on him to press their views. Some abolitionists asked him to pursue a more aggressive attack on slavery, some black community groups demanded that he take a stronger stand against African colonization, and the American Colonization Society wanted him to reconsider his views about their resettlement program.

Unsure of the best way to foster black progress, Russwurm became more willing than ever before to listen to ideas that he had previously disregarded. When members of the American Colonization Society approached him in early 1829 in the hope of gaining his support, he was fairly receptive to their views. The society had tried to convince him of the value of their plan for free blacks during his emergence as one of New York's black leaders, but the attempt had been flatly rejected. The group's renewed attempt to win him over came at a time when he was being sniped at by radical black leaders and when he

was no longer dominated by the strong-willed Cornish.

The colonization society's members were confident that they could sway Russwurm to their side. The colonizationists knew he was struggling to set his own course and was open to influence. They discussed their proposals with him, trying hard to prove that their organization offered blacks their best opportunity for dignity and freedom. Denying the abolitionists' charge that the society was trying to weaken the antislavery movement, the colonizationists insisted that slaveowners were more likely to free a slave who wanted to move to Liberia. Indeed, some slaveowners had freed slaves on the condition that they emigrate abroad.

Opponents of the American Colonization Society accused it of taking unfair advantage of Russwurm while he was harried and overworked, but although he may have been open to persuasion, he was never

Whip-cracking colonization society officials herd freed slaves aboard a Liberia-bound ship in this cartoon from an abolitionist journal, sarcastically captioned " 'Nuisances' going as 'missionaries,' 'with their own consent.' "

THE

COLONIZATION SCHEME CONSIDERED,

IN

ITS REJECTION BY THE COLORED PEOPLE—IN ITS

TENDENCY TO UPHOLD CASTE—IN ITS

UNFITNESS FOR CHRISTIANIZING AND CIVILIZING

THE ABORIGINES OF AFRICA,

AND FOR PUTTING A STOP TO

THE AFRICAN SLAVE TRADE:

IN A LETTER TO

THE HON. THEODORE FRELINGHUYSEN

AND

THE HON. BENJAMIN F. BUTLER;

BY

SAMUEL E. CORNISH AND THEODORE S. WRIGHT,

PASTORS OF THE COLORED PRESBYTERIAN CHURCHES IN THE CITIES OF
NEWARK AND NEW YORK.

NEWARK:
PRINTED BY AARON GUEST, 121 MARKET-STREET.

1840.

Russwurm's support for the American Colonization Society's resettlement program was not shared by most of his newspaper's readers or by his former partner, Samuel Cornish, who later published pamphlets attacking the colonization movement.

foolish. Only an overriding belief that the colonizationists' ideas offered the best hope for blacks could have attracted him to their movement. Never one to make quick judgments, Russwurm took his time and investigated all sides of the issue before making his decision.

Russwurm was well aware of the failures and problems of the colonization society. He knew that only a handful of blacks had emigrated to Africa—*Freedom's Journal* had published the exact figures. He was not deaf to the rumors that Liberia's settlers were having a rough time in their new home. He heard reports that prospective settlers had chosen to remain in slavery rather than risk the hardships of colonization. He also knew that some supporters of the colonization movement were bigots who had the interests of white slaveowners—rather than the interests of blacks—at heart.

Russwurm saw that the American Colonization Society had many faults, but he also believed that there were many critical issues the abolitionists ignored. Many of the abolitionists had given little thought to what would happen to the 2 million poor and uneducated slaves if complete emancipation was carried out in America. Where would the freed slaves go? he asked. How could they expect to earn a decent living when white society thwarted their attempts to improve their lives?

Russwurm maintained that many antislavery fighters held overly optimistic views about the readiness of white Americans to accept large numbers of free blacks. He asked the abolitionists, "If the slaves of our country with one word were delivered from bondage, can they be elevated to an equality with the whites? Can they, while in this country be divested of the odium of inferior and degraded caste?"

Russwurm had another major objection to the abolitionists: Many of their plans to abolish slavery involved violence, something he felt should be avoided at all costs. Attacks on slaveowners would only provoke retaliation against slaves.

Russwurm knew that the South would never give up its cherished slave system without a bloody struggle. He wrote in his newspaper, "We have not the

Abolitionist leaders (left to right) William Lloyd Garrison, George Thompson, and Wendell Phillips were vehement opponents of the American Colonization Society. Outraged by Russwurm's defense of the colonization movement, Garrison described him as "suffused with shame and branded with the stigma of disgrace."

least hope, that slavery on the abolitionist plan, is at all likely to be terminated without violence of the most appalling character; we have little thought that we can be indifferent to the consequences without deep and aggravated guilt."

As Russwurm pondered the issue, he became more and more convinced that the critics of colonization could not offer any practical solution to the problems confronting blacks. His aversion to violence and his hope that blacks could be free without having to die for their freedom ultimately turned him in the direction of the American Colonization Society. Colonization seemed to offer a reasonable course that would guarantee a peaceful separation of blacks from a nation that would never fully accept them as equal citizens. "This plan," he said, "has another advantage in doing no violence to the feelings or principles of master or servant. It sends them with their own consent, and violence is unknown, so that no bad feelings are awakened."

Early in 1829, readers of *Freedom's Journal* began to notice a gradual change in the tone of the articles Russwurm wrote about colonization. All material criticizing the American Colonization Society disappeared. In three separate places in one February issue, he openly defended colonization. He wrote that the colonization society was laying a good foundation for blacks in Liberia, and he wished the people settling there good luck. He announced that *Freedom's Journal* was changing its position on colonization. He cited the society for having the best program available for blacks and labeled his earlier views about the organization as "mistaken."

Subsequent issues of the newspaper brought more of the same sentiment. In the March 7 periodical, Russwurm admitted that hardships faced the settlers in Liberia yet firmly defended his change in position. In the next issue, he proclaimed his admiration for

WALKER'S

APPEAL,

IN FOUR ARTICLES,

TOGETHER WITH

A PREAMBLE,

TO THE

COLORED CITIZENS OF THE WORLD,

BUT IN PARTICULAR, AND VERY EXPRESSLY TO THOSE OF THE

UNITED STATES OF AMERICA.

Written in Boston, in the State of Massachusetts, Sept. 28, 1829.

SECOND EDITION, WITH CORRECTIONS, &c.

BY DAVID WALKER.

1830.

the supporters of colonization and insisted that because colonization would speed emancipation, it was the best strategy for black Americans.

The majority of the people who read *Freedom's Journal* were outraged by Russwurm's dramatic change of heart. He was deluged with hate mail, much of it accusing him of selling out to the colonizationists and betraying the race that had supported him in launching his newspaper. A spokesman for a group of angry blacks stated, "Before God, we know of no surer burial place than Africa for men of any color; that we will never envy John B. Russwurm his ambition; and that we will pray God, that his notions of nobleness may never enter our hearts."

Black abolitionist David Walker's Appeal—a call for violent black revolution—aroused a storm of controversy throughout the United States when it was published in 1829. Urging slaves to stand up to their masters and "kill or be killed," Walker warned whites: "Remember Americans, that we must and shall be free and enlightened as you are. . . . God will deliver us from under you."

In September 1829, Russwurm set sail from New York harbor on a ship bound for Liberia. Despite the abuse he had suffered because of his unpopular stand on colonization, he remained convinced that Africa was the place where black Americans should pursue their quest for freedom.

The attacks on Russwurm came from every part of the black community. People who had once praised him now watched with satisfaction as he was burned in effigy. To the black community, he had become the most hypocritical of traitors.

Russwurm's transformation into a social pariah occurred in the same year that David Walker, a former slave who had become a sales agent for *Freedom's Journal*, issued an electrifying challenge to the system that had stripped him of his human dignity. In a document that became known as *Walker's Appeal*, the radical abolitionist from Boston called on slaves to strike back against their masters. He told blacks, "America is more our country than it is the whites— we have enriched it with our blood and tears." Prophesying an awful fate for white Americans, he warned them, "You will yet curse the day you were ever born."

Russwurm was not swayed by the fiery visions called forth by radical abolitionists such as Walker. Instead, he held to his unpopular views. He humbly explained, "We now stand before the community, a feeble advocate of the Society. We have carefully examined the different plans now in operation for our benefit, and none, we believe, can reach half so efficiently the masses as the plan of colonization on the West coast of Africa."

No explanation could quiet Russwurm's critics, however, and they demanded that he resign from *Freedom's Journal.* On March 28, 1829, two years after the release of the first issue of the newspaper, he bowed to public pressure and gave up his position. Publication of the newspaper was suspended for two months, until it was revived briefly by Samuel Cornish under the title *The Rights of All.*

Wishing to escape from the furor that surrounded him, Russwurm left New York City and went back to Bowdoin College. There he began studying for an advanced degree. Then the American Colonization Society offered him a job as superintendent of schools in Liberia, an assignment that was too tempting to refuse.

In the three tumultuous years that separated Russwurm's graduation from college and his departure for Africa in September 1829, he had been both a hero and a scoundrel to blacks. His experiences had confirmed his belief that blacks must find their own place in the world free of the racial hatred that put such heavy restraints on the black community in America. He was hoping that place might be Liberia.

6
LIBERTY'S SHADOW

❧

As THE DISTANCE separating Russwurm from America grew ever wider on the voyage to West Africa, he gradually stopped thinking about the conflict he had left behind and began planning for life in Liberia. His thoughts went far beyond the scope of his job as superintendent of schools for the infant colony: He hoped to found a newspaper there and help the black settlers establish a commanding voice in their own affairs. The possibilities for progress now seemed limitless to him.

Russwurm's first reaction to Liberia was overwhelmingly positive. He arrived in the colony's capital, the port town of Monrovia, on November 15, 1829, and immediately wrote to his relatives in America. "What my sensations were upon landing I can hardly describe," he told them, full of enthusiasm for his new home. He noted that Monrovia was larger and more prosperous than he had expected and exclaimed triumphantly, "You here behold coloured men exercising all the duties of offices of which you can scarcely believe, many fulfill the important duties with much dignity. We have here a republic in miniature."

Russwurm's travel-weary eyes had deceived him, however. He soon began to realize that the situation

Russwurm arrived at the Liberian capital, Monrovia, in November 1829 and discovered, he said, a black "republic in miniature." He quickly learned that he was mistaken.

67

in Liberia was far less pleasant than he had first thought. Monrovia's impressive-looking stone government buildings and sturdy little settlers' houses hid ugly truths that were revealed to him only after he had lived in the colony for a while.

Liberia, at the time of Russwurm's arrival, was still a raw pioneering outpost of a few hundred settlers located in a section of West Africa known as the Grain Coast. To the north of Liberia was Sierra Leone, a colony founded in 1787 by the British as a refuge for freed slaves. Five hundred miles to the east of Liberia was the Slave Coast, an area that had been especially notorious in earlier times as a center of the slave trade.

The first group of settlers organized by the American Colonization Society had sailed from New York to Sierra Leone in early 1820, but disease and dissension had combined to wipe out the expedition before any of the members reached their destination. Two years later, a settlement was established along the Liberian coast on land bought from local tribes. After holding a day of thanksgiving, the colonists set about the hard task of squeezing a living out of the dense forests and winding river valleys of their new land.

Liberia was only seven years old when Russwurm moved there, and the colony's settlers were just beginning to carve out a home for themselves in the dense forests and disease-ridden swamps of the West African coast. Shown here is a street in Monrovia as it looked a few decades later, at a time when the colony had become more prosperous.

From the beginning, Liberia was torn by disputes between its black settlers and the white officials sent by the American Colonization Society to administer the colony. During most of Liberia's first six years of existence, its colonial agent—the highest-ranking governing official—was an enterprising man named Jehudi Ashmun, who unfortunately paid little attention to the needs of the settlers. Rallying around the Baptist minister Lott Cary and other educated black leaders, the settlers demanded that they be given a voice in the colony's affairs. However, they were hampered by their total dependence on funds and supplies sent by the colonization society, and their campaign for self-government made little headway.

When Russwurm took up his duties as supervisor of Liberia's educational system, he learned—to his anger and great disappointment—just how little power the black colonists had. No blacks had yet been appointed to the highest leadership positions in Liberia, and they were treated as wards of the colony who were incapable of making important decisions. The settlers were allowed to elect members of their community to some government positions, but the selections had to be approved by the colonial agent.

To Russwurm, the racial situation in his new home seemed depressingly similar to the one he had escaped from in America. In Liberia, however, there was one big difference. Nearly the entire population was black.

The problems between the settlers and the colonial agents were only part of the troubles that Russwurm encountered when he moved to Liberia. The tropical climate in the area was a severe test for even the hardiest settlers, with torrential rains blanketing the coast for one-half of the year and dry weather predominating in the other half. Malaria and other lethal diseases took a huge toll on the residents and left many families without any productive workers.

Liberia's black settlers were allowed only a minimal role in government and had tense relations with most of the white officials whom the American Colonization Society appointed to administer the colony. Jehudi Ashmun (shown here) governed the colony during its early years.

Farming, the colony's chief industry, was grueling work because forested areas first had to be cleared so crops could be planted. The settlers were hampered in the early years by a shortage of tools. In time, though, they learned to coax plentiful harvests of rice, sweet potatoes, beans, and other crops from the infertile soil.

To add to these difficulties, the native African peoples resented the presence of settlers in the area. More than 20 tribes—including the Mandingo, Bassa, and Kru—occupied the region surrounding the settlement at Monrovia, and they did not welcome intruders, black or white. The Africans regarded the black Americans as "whites" because the settlers—many of whom were as light-skinned as Russwurm—dressed, spoke, and lived like white men. The colonists carried on a thriving trade with the natives during times of peace, but disputes between the two groups sometimes erupted into open warfare.

One of the chief points of conflict between the colony and the natives was the slave trade. As Russwurm learned to his disgust when he arrived in Lib-

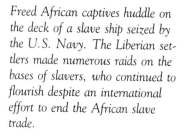

Freed African captives huddle on the deck of a slave ship seized by the U.S. Navy. The Liberian settlers made numerous raids on the bases of slavers, who continued to flourish despite an international effort to end the African slave trade.

eria, many of the local tribes sold war captives to slave traders, who smuggled their human cargoes into American and West Indian ports at a tremendous profit. The Liberians raided numerous slave depots and freed the captives, but these actions sparked off retaliatory attacks from the tribes that depended on the trade.

The taunts of Russwurm's American critics were ringing in his ears as he began his work in Liberia. The stories he had heard about the harsh conditions in the colony had been true, and blacks had no more control over their own lives than they had in the United States. Yet Russwurm refused to be discouraged by what he saw. He knew that the settlers' lives could be vastly improved with a united community effort led by resolute and practical leaders. In addition, the American Colonization Society was having difficulty in finding capable white officials to govern Liberia; Russwurm was certain that blacks would

West African tribesmen stand next to a hut containing religious idols known as fetishes. The natives living near Liberia regarded the black colonists as white because they had light-colored skin and wore American-style clothing.

eventually be appointed to the colony's highest positions.

The first colonial agent whom Russwurm encountered was Joseph Mechlin. Extremely bigoted, he was determined to keep blacks—whom he looked upon as his "charges"—from gaining any position of influence in the colony. Russwurm immediately set out to increase his own standing in the community, believing, as always, that the best way to change negative stereotypes about blacks was to prove by example that blacks were not an inferior race.

As superintendent of education, Russwurm quickly became a visible force in the colony. During his visits to families in Monrovia, he talked to parents about the importance of having their children attend classes on a regular basis. His optimism and high spirits endeared him to community members, who soon realized that he was a man who could get things done.

It was through his efforts to improve the quality of education in the colony that Russwurm became friendly with George McGill, a minister who had come to Liberia with his wife and children two years before. From 1827 to 1829, McGill had served as the director of education and had worked hard to improve the colony's primitive school system. Upon meeting Russwurm, he took an instant liking to his bright young successor and became his friend and adviser.

While Russwurm worked to expand the school system, he also began making plans to establish a newspaper in the colony. Despite the lack of many goods and services in Liberia, the colony owned a printing press. A gift from the people of Boston, the press had been used briefly to print issues of the colony's first newspaper, the *Liberia Herald.* After the death of the newspaper's editor, Charles Force, publication was discontinued because no other settler knew how to operate the machine.

Russwurm decided to step into Force's shoes and continue the newspaper under the same name. In March 1830—four months after his arrival in Monrovia and exactly three years after the birth of *Freedom's Journal*—he put out the first issue of the revived *Liberia Herald*. The paper proved to be a welcome sight to the frustrated black Americans who had made the perilous journey to Africa only to find that they still had no voice of their own. Both blacks and whites in the colony praised Russwurm and the *Liberia Herald*.

Even Mechlin was impressed. In a report to the headquarters of the American Colonization Society, the colonial agent wrote, "I send you something which will no doubt excite agreeable surprise—that is, 300 copies of the first number of the *Liberia Herald*, just issued from the press. . . . This, I am in hope, will show to the people at home that we are making greater progress than they are willing to give us credit for."

Mechlin was unusually complimentary to the *Liberia Herald*'s black editor, whom he described in a letter to the American Colonization Society as a "great acquisition" for the colonial administration. Although Russwurm deeply resented Mechlin's attitude toward the settlers, he was glad to be on good terms with the colonial agent. In his typically diplomatic manner, he began to walk the line that separated the black and white worlds.

Russwurm was elected colonial secretary by the black community a few months after he began publishing the *Liberia Herald*. This position—which in the past had been held by a white—gave him responsibility for the colony's records and correspondence and allowed him access to the highest officials of the American Colonization Society in the United States. Armed with his new title, he believed that he could lead the battle for reforms that would guar-

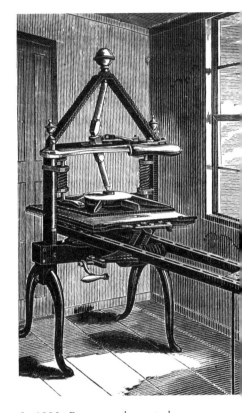

In 1830, Russwurm began publishing the Liberia Herald. *Besides providing the colonists with news of local events and the outside world, the newspaper helped unite the colony during its troubled early years. The machine shown here is typical of the kind of presses used to print newspapers in the mid-1800s.*

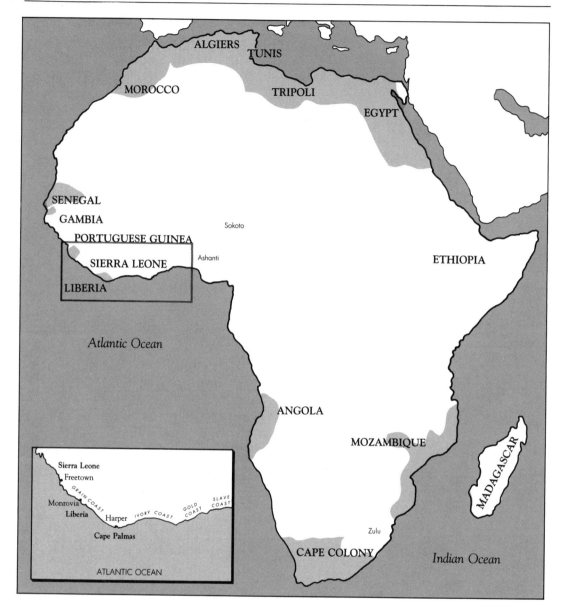

A map of Africa as it appeared in the 1830s highlights the part of the West African coast on which the colony of Liberia was established.

antee the settlers a controlling vote over their own affairs.

The reforms never came. Russwurm tried to work closely with Liberia's white leaders, but the colony's racial situation remained as it was. In addition, Mechlin and his officers began to fear that Russwurm was gaining too much power and restricted his responsibilities.

Russwurm's patience with the white officials—whom he described to his friends as filled with "fanaticism, bigotry and ignorance"—started to wear thin. As tensions between the settlers and the government continued to grow, he found that his position as colonial secretary placed him at the center of the conflict. He turned to his friends for support. He spent an especially large amount of time at the home of George McGill, where he got to know McGill's attractive daughter, Sarah. After courting Sarah in the formal style of the time, he asked for her hand in marriage and was accepted. The two were married in 1833.

Russwurm had finally found a remedy for the loneliness that had plagued him since leaving his friends and family behind in America. But his marriage also forced him to look for additional ways to make money, for he realized that he could not support a family on his current income. Soon after his wedding, he formed a partnership in a trading business with a colonist named Joseph Dailey. Russwurm announced the new venture in the *Liberia Herald*, advertising to readers the sale of a cargo of tobacco, pork, nails, soap, and other provisions.

Unfortunately for Russwurm, the founding of his business venture coincided with the beginning of warfare between the Liberians and local tribes. The colony's economy was hurt, and Russwurm and Dailey had to take a sharp loss on the sale of their goods. The failure of the business was especially bitter to

Although Russwurm's attempt to establish himself as a merchant was a costly failure, some Liberians became wealthy by exporting palm oil to the American market. In the 1800s, oil pressed from the nuts harvested from palm trees was used to make soap, candles, and industrial lubricating greases.

Russwurm because it prevented him from making a trip he had been planning to the United States.

In Russwurm's letters to his half brother Francis, he wrote about being homesick for Maine but gave little indication of the great hardships that he and most of the other settlers had to endure in Liberia. Joseph Dailey, on the other hand, wrote in his letters that conditions in the colony were "deplorable," and he expressed concern over his own health as well as Russwurm's. He described Russwurm as being emaciated beyond recognition.

Russwurm was reluctant to admit that his decision to support the American Colonization Society might have been a mistake and that his dream of finding freedom in Liberia had turned into a nightmare. He still clung to his hope that a black would be appointed to govern the colony. When Joseph Mechlin was at last forced to resign from his position in 1834, Russwurm and other settlers urged the colonization society to choose a successor to the colonial agent from among the leaders of Liberia's black community. Many thought that the person should be Russwurm.

Instead, the colonization society chose another white colonial agent, the Reverend John Pinney, a Baptist minister who had never been to Liberia and had little awareness of the needs of the black community. Worse, Pinney had openly stated that his education "had induced him to be prejudiced against colored persons." Russwurm's disappointment over the selection turned to rage when the new agent neglected the black community and instead devoted his energies to preaching to the natives.

Pinney's incompetence and arrogance finally drove the settlers into open defiance of the government. Organizing behind two militant leaders, Hiliary Teage and Jacob Prout, a group of blacks seized control of Monrovia's courthouse during the middle of a trial. Shouting their objections to Pinney's administration, they demanded that the colonial agent resign.

Pinney responded by issuing a proclamation that the colonists were in a state of illegal rebellion. He ordered Russwurm to print the statement in the *Liberia Herald*. Knowing that the proclamation would enrage the colonists and spark off more violent confrontations, Russwurm tried to persuade Pinney to change his mind. When his protests were ignored, Russwurm was left with an agonizing dilemma: If he followed Pinney's order, the settlers would accuse him of betraying them; if he disobeyed the order, his newspaper would be shut down. Praying that his fellow settlers would understand his position, he chose to print the statement.

The response from the black community was worse than Russwurm expected. Shouting that he should have stood up to Pinney, an angry mob stormed the office of the *Liberia Herald*. Russwurm barely managed to talk the rioters out of destroying the printing press.

An African king receives Bible instruction from Christian missionaries. During Russwurm's term as colonial secretary, he was angered that some of the white ministers appointed to govern Liberia were more interested in converting native tribes to Christianity than in attending to the colonists' pressing needs for better housing and medical care.

Russwurm gradually mended his relations with the black community, but the incident damaged his morale and his already frail health. Furious about all the trouble that Pinney had caused in Liberia, Russwurm wrote a letter of protest to the American Colonization Society. Describing the intolerable position he had been put in because of the colonial agent's arrogance, Russwurm complained, "The whole blame has been cast upon me." He added as a word of warning, "I have suffered so much persecution that I am almost tempted to abandon all and flee."

In the face of the settlers' continuing resistance to government authority, Pinney resigned his office. Russwurm and his black colleagues were passed over once again by the colonization society, which appointed another white minister, Ezekiel Skinner, to govern the colony. The colonization society also reached another decision: Rather than address the settlers' demands for more political rights and greater economic assistance, it further restricted what little part blacks had in the government.

Guadillar Farm, a village to the north of Monrovia. Liberia expanded inland and along the coast as the flow of American settlers to the colony continued in the 1830s. By 1835, however, Russwurm had resolved to leave Liberia because of the American Colonization Society's refusal to appoint blacks to positions of leadership.

Russwurm's letters to the society had been in vain. In fact, the society, believing he was a threat to the colonial administration, reduced the responsibilities of the colonial secretary post. Russwurm's election as colonial secretary had meant little in terms of real power for blacks, yet the position had been a symbol to the colonists of their right to have their own elected representative in the government. Now even that right had been taken away.

Russwurm's frustrations increased as the colonization society continued to whittle away at his position in the colony. Next, it attacked his control of the *Liberia Herald*. He was directed to accept "editorial assistance" from Skinner, which in effect meant that every word he wrote could be censored by the colonial agent.

Russwurm made a final effort to restore his position by running for vice-agent, the highest elective office still open to blacks. He won the election, but Skinner refused to allow him to take office. This was the final blow for Russwurm. The struggle with the colonization society had exhausted him and left him in poor health. In addition, he was now burdened with increased family responsibilities: Sarah Russwurm had recently given birth to their first child, whom she named George, after her father.

In September 1835, Russwurm wrote to his half brother Francis that he was ready to admit that his association with the American Colonization Society had been an error. "I suppose I shall live and die in Africa," he said, "but I hope not in Liberia." Six years had passed since his ship had docked in Monrovia, and his hopes of finding in Liberia a home where blacks could live in freedom and dignity had been shattered.

It was time to search elsewhere for the elusive land of liberty.

7
GOVERNOR OF A FREE PEOPLE

❦

RUSSWURM WAS BUSY rethinking his decision to move to Africa when he embarked on his quest for a new home. His experiences in Liberia had left him somewhat disillusioned, and so he now had to face some difficult questions. Had he been chasing vainly after a dream of liberty when he settled in the colony? Would his time have been better spent if he had stayed in the United States and helped lead the struggle for black freedom?

In the six years that Russwurm had lived in Liberia, from 1829 to 1835, he had been following developments in the United States from the newspapers and letters sent to him by American friends. He knew that the political atmosphere in the United States had grown increasingly tense as abolitionist groups had pushed the debate over slavery into the center of national attention. Wealthy southern slave owners continued to argue that slavery was crucial to the health of the nation's economy and should be allowed to grow; abolitionists declared that slavery was immoral and should be eliminated immediately

A view of the town of Harper in the Maryland Colony, a settlement founded near Liberia by the Maryland Colonization Society. In 1835, Russwurm became interested in moving to the new colony after he learned that the blacks who settled there were protected by a bill of rights.

81

if the United States was to live up to its claim of being the "land of liberty." The dispute raged on with no hope for a solution in sight, and violent clashes between proslavery and antislavery advocates occurred with increasing frequency.

While Russwurm was living in Liberia, one of his former critics, William Lloyd Garrison, was braving hostile crowds to speak out against slavery. Garrison's newspaper, the *Liberator*, was among the numerous antislavery journals that followed in the footsteps of *Freedom's Journal*. Russwurm's former partner, Samuel Cornish, was also active in the crusade against slavery. Besides publishing *The Colored American*, a militant abolitionist journal, Cornish attended many national conventions of black leaders that were organized during this period.

While Garrison and Cornish used words to stir up opposition to slavery, some antislavery leaders turned to the sword. In August 1831, a slave preacher named Nat Turner organized one of the bloodiest slave uprisings in American history. Maintaining that God had chosen him to guide his people to freedom,

While living in Africa, Russwurm kept informed about the struggle for black freedom in America. Among the most noteworthy events of the time was the bloody slave revolt led by Nat Turner (second from left) in Virginia in 1831.

In the mid-1800s, abolitionist conventions helped arouse international protests against the evils of slavery. Shown here is a meeting that took place in London in 1840.

Turner led a group of Virginia slaves in a ferocious, two-day attack on their masters. Before the revolt was suppressed and Turner was caught and hanged, more than 50 whites had been cut down by the rebels. About 120 blacks were slaughtered by whites in retaliation.

Frightened by Turner's uprising, the governments of the southern states rushed to prevent the flame of revolt from spreading. New laws restricted slaves from meeting together and decreed brutal punishments for even minor offenses, such as leaving a cow unattended. Antislavery groups were silenced in the South by laws that made it a crime to distribute abolitionist literature there.

But laws and censorship could not suppress the slavery issue. More and more, the United States stood alone in its acceptance of slavery. When Great Britain outlawed slavery within all of its colonies in 1832, great pressure was placed on America to alter its position on slavery as well.

Russwurm was saddened by the situation in America, but he could at least take comfort in arguing that he had made the right decision by moving to Africa. Liberians lived in a condition of great poverty and hardship and were ruled by white leaders, but at no time did they suffer the kind of racial abuse that black Americans endured. One of Russwurm's fellow settlers expressed his satisfaction with life in Africa when he wrote to an American friend, "If any of my friends enquire about me tell them I am under my own vine and fig tree [where] none dare molest me nor make me afraid." Another colonist proudly wrote, "Africa is the land of freedom. . . . This is the land of our forefathers, destined to be the home of their descendants."

Russwurm continued to defend the principles of the African colonization movement. It was the directors of the American Colonization Society with whom he had problems. He was sure that if he could work with a colonizing organization that was less racially prejudiced, the dream of black self-government might still be realized.

By 1836, a number of branches of the American Colonization Society had broken away from the parent organization and launched efforts to start separate settlements near Monrovia. Russwurm was particularly interested in one of these groups, the Maryland Society, which had already established a colony that was a short distance from Liberia. Rather ironically, it was the long shadow of Nat Turner that was responsible for the Maryland Society's success. After his slave revolt in Virginia, white Marylanders were afraid that similar uprisings might occur in their own state and decided that the best way to deal with the threat was to relieve their state of its large population of free blacks by supporting the colonization movement. In 1832, Maryland became the first state to adopt colonization as an official policy and approved a large grant of money for the Maryland Society.

Russwurm knew that the motivations of the Maryland Society were rooted in racism, but he was more concerned about how the organization would treat the colonists it resettled in Africa. In early 1834, when the Maryland Society sent its first expedition to West Africa, he greeted the colonists and their leader, James Hall, as they arrived for a short stay in Monrovia. He was glad to learn that Dr. Hall, a white Bowdoin alumnus and a man he deeply respected, had been chosen to found the new colony.

Russwurm had met Hall two years earlier when the doctor had been practicing medicine in Liberia. He knew that Hall had a good understanding of the needs and problems of the settlers as well as of the natives. After talking with Hall and learning that the Maryland Society had promised the settlers a leading voice in deciding their own destiny, Russwurm thought about moving to the new colony.

When Hall's expedition left Monrovia, it sailed southward down the West African coast until it reached a place called Cape Palmas. Hall had become friendly with the native tribes during a previous visit to the area, and he used his good reputation with them to negotiate for land. Using such currency as brass-barreled pistols, cocked hats, and fishhooks, the doctor purchased approximately 800 square miles of land from the local chieftains and established the Maryland Colony. The one type of merchandise with which Hall refused to trade was alcohol, which slave traders commonly used to buy their human cargoes.

A native village on the coast of Cape Palmas. To buy the land on which Maryland Colony was founded, the settlers paid the local tribes an assortment of guns and feathered hats.

From the beginning, the Maryland Colony was set up differently from Liberia. The president of the Maryland Society, John Latrobe, and his colleagues were wise enough to learn from the mistakes made in the older colony. First, the settlers at Cape Palmas were given a constitution, complete with a bill of rights that guaranteed them the opportunity to participate in the colony's government. Furthermore, the Maryland Colony's economy was to depend mainly on its agriculture rather than on trading with the natives. This policy was established because many of the troubles between the Liberians and native tribes had been caused by trade disputes, and unscrupulous colonists sometimes used alcohol to intoxicate and then cheat the natives.

As Russwurm watched the developments in the Maryland Colony, he became excited that a group of black Americans finally had the chance to develop

John Latrobe, the president of the Maryland Colonization Society, believed that black colonists in West Africa should be allowed to govern themselves. Impressed by reports of Russwurm's work in Liberia, Latrobe's organization offered him the position of governor of Maryland Colony.

their own community. Only one major component was still missing—a black leader.

Fortunately, the Maryland Society recognized that many of the problems in Liberia had existed because whites had been appointed to govern the black settlers. When Hall, exhausted from his pioneering work, returned to the United States in 1836, he recommended Russwurm for the position of governor at Cape Palmas. The Maryland Society offered him the post, impressed by the doctor's high praise for Russwurm's abilities.

The timing could not have been better for Russwurm, who desperately wanted to leave Liberia. Here, at last, was the opportunity upon which he had hung his hopes and dreams. In 1836, with his wife and two sons (the second of whom was named James, after Dr. Hall), he took up residence in the official government house at Harper, the principal town of the Maryland Colony.

Russwurm was proud to be the governor of the black community at Cape Palmas. He was also fully aware that the position was a difficult one to fill. As the first black high official appointed by an all-white organization, he had the responsibility of proving that a black man was capable of exercising the type of judgment and leadership needed to administer a struggling colony. Sure of his ability to handle the job, he wrote to the Maryland Society that "the greatest stimulus ever presented to a man of color in the United States has been the promotion of men of his race to the office of great trust and responsibility."

After taking office, Russwurm immediately tackled the enormous task of turning the scattered settlements in Cape Palmas's malaria-ridden jungles into a well-managed colony. At first, he faced numerous challenges to his authority. He had special difficulties with the officers of the U.S. Navy ships that stopped at Cape Palmas to deliver supplies. Unused to dealing

Russwurm's years of experience on the coast of West Africa were of immense value to the colonists at Cape Palmas. While serving as governor, he spent most of his time at the town of Harper, shown here as it appeared about 30 years later.

with a black person on equal terms, the naval officers refused to confer with him on an official basis. Russwurm handled the unpleasant situation with patience and diplomacy, often using white missionaries or doctors as intermediaries.

Totally dedicated to the welfare of the settlers at Cape Palmas, Russwurm concerned himself with every aspect of the developing colony. He was not just a governor but also the chief justice of the law court, supervisor of the educational system, and commander of the colony's guards. His guidance was critical for a group of people who had been thrown together in an unfamiliar land and who had little education and no experience in governing themselves. Russwurm intended to prove that any people who were given self-respect, education, occupational training, and a chance to improve themselves could build a thriving community.

It was Russwurm's responsibility as governor to decide how to distribute the supplies that the Maryland Society sent to the colony twice a year. These supplies, which were kept in the Cape Palmas Agency Store at the Harper settlement, were not enough to support the colony. Russwurm knew that the settlers had to become industrious farmers if the colony was to survive.

Russwurm's efforts to turn the Maryland Colony into a self-sufficient agricultural community met with resistance from the settlers at first. Each colonist was granted a plot of land to farm, but only a handful had farming experience and all had difficulty with the hot climate and poor soil of the West African coast. Some people took advantage of the Maryland Society's pledge to support all new settlers during their first six months and tried to continue the arrangement indefinitely.

Russwurm had read books on agricultural science and had studied farming methods used by the settlers in Liberia. At Cape Palmas, he devoted much of his time to training the colonists how to work the land so that they could produce corn, tobacco, and cotton and harvest native crops such as oil-producing palm trees. He became disappointed and somewhat angry that so few of the colonists were willing to work hard at developing their own land. Eventually, he used his power as governor to institute a law that required colonists to cultivate at least one acre in order to be eligible to receive supplies from the colony store.

Russwurm's policies eventually succeeded in making the colony much more independent of support from overseas. The Cape Palmas settlers became more skilled at coaxing eggplants and peanuts to grow in their fields, and the colony gradually expanded and established new towns further inland. Pleased with the colony's progress, Russwurm wrote in a letter to President Latrobe of the Maryland Society that with "a little pinching and scolding," most of the colonists had taken to farming. "We are creeping ahead every year, with a steady pace," he reported optimistically.

Seemingly involved in every activity in Maryland Colony, Russwurm pushed himself so hard that he exhausted himself and put his health at great risk.

But he did not face his duties alone. His chief assistant was his brother-in-law, Samuel McGill, the first black American physician in the West African colonies. McGill labored heroically to improve the colony's sanitary conditions and to establish medical facilities. Besides McGill and other members of the colony's governing council, there was a small corps of trained carpenters, masons, and tanners whom Russwurm looked to for advice on how to build the colony.

A longtime champion of education, Russwurm gave special attention to the colony's school system. When he arrived at Cape Palmas, he found that the one school in the Harper settlement was "in a drooping state," he said, troubled by poor attendance and a lack of qualified teachers. As he had done in Liberia, he spent much time urging parents to keep their children in the classroom. Within a year, he had restored life to the school. He then established another school near the towns further inland.

The colony's school system began to take shape with the help of money and supplies sent by the Maryland Society and various church groups. Finding competent teachers was always difficult, however, and Russwurm sometimes discovered that the people sent from America to teach in the schools were practically illiterate. He was also forced to admit that the majority of the students "think it all sufficient, if they can stammer through a book and scratch their names on paper." Nevertheless, he was pleased to note that many of the schools' female students did exceptionally well.

Russwurm hoped that the colony's school system would eventually help bring about an improvement in the behavior of its citizens. Theft and prostitution were constant problems in the Cape Palmas settlements, and it was Russwurm's responsibility as chief justice to oversee the legal system. Deeply upset about the lax morals of young female offenders who were

brought before him, he ordered the construction of a special building to serve as a residence for homeless single women "as a prevention to their acquiring loose and vicious habits." Despite this attempt, Russwurm had little success in making a dent in criminal activities until 1843, when a stone jail was built in Harper.

Maintaining friendly relations with the area's native tribes was another duty that occupied much of Russwurm's time. As in Liberia, the natives viewed the colonists as white American strangers rather than as black Africans. Because the settlers were outnumbered by more than three to one, the colony's safety depended on its governor's ability to smooth over

A native village in West Africa. The Cape Palmas colonists depended on neighboring tribes for much of their food supply, and Russwurm worked hard to maintain friendly relations with local chiefs.

disputes with the Africans. Russwurm frequently called on local chieftains to pay his respects and seek out their good will.

Many of the tribal peoples around Cape Palmas asked Russwurm to build schools on their land so their children could learn the mysteries of reading and writing. Russwurm was happy to oblige, and with the help of missionaries he established half a dozen schools for African students. Some problems developed when Russwurm insisted that the fathers of the schools' female students sign a pledge swearing that they would not sell their daughters or force them to marry against their wishes. Because African fathers regarded their daughters as property to be bought and sold, they were reluctant to allow the girls to go to school.

Maryland Colony's founders had hoped that the settlers would not have to depend on trading with the natives to survive. Because of their limited success with farming, however, buying grains, meats, and fruits from the local tribes became a necessity. Unfortunately, the colony had no official currency to use in trading with the Africans, and the settlers were forced to use packets of cotton or tobacco as money. This type of currency was not always acceptable to the natives, who preferred to receive expensive manufactured goods that were always in short supply at the colony's store.

In 1839, Russwurm decided to resolve the colony's currency problems once and for all. He proposed to the Maryland Society's board of managers that it issue paper certificates that could be redeemed for goods at the Cape Palmas Agency Store. The board was enthusiastic about the idea and had bills printed that were stamped with distinctive, easily recognizable pictures so that the non–English-speaking natives would be able to comprehend their value.

Jubilant about the success of his effort to establish a standard currency in the colony, Russwurm declared that his next projects would include the founding of a savings bank and a health insurance organization. Meanwhile, he had to take steps to strengthen the colony's economy, because by 1840 the directors of the Maryland Society had become convinced that the colony was almost ready to survive on its own. They wrote to Russwurm that the settlers would have to assume a much larger share of the burden of supporting themselves.

Russwurm met the challenge with his usual resolve. Through trade and taxation, he increased the resources of the colonial treasury and contributed funds for the erection of public buildings and the purchase of the semiannual supply shipments sent by the Maryland Society. In 1840, he paid for all the goods delivered to the colony store with a shipment of palm oil.

Bit by bit, Russwurm was building Maryland Colony into a vigorous community of free black people. In the face of great skepticism, the colonists were proving that blacks could create their own society and govern their own affairs. Now one more question remained for Russwurm: Were the American colonies in West Africa ready for independence? ❧

8

THE LOVE
OF LIBERTY

WHILE HE LIVED in Liberia and Maryland Colony, Russwurm constantly pressed for the right of black colonists in Africa to govern themselves and create their own society free of white interference. In September 1841, he received news from Monrovia that gave him hope that the time of black self-rule in West Africa was finally at hand. The American Colonization Society, bowing to the inevitable in the face of continuing strife between Liberia's settlers and white administrators, appointed a wealthy black merchant named Joseph Roberts as governor of Liberia.

Roberts's appointment as head of the government in Monrovia was an important step toward the foundation of an independent black nation in West Africa. Like Maryland Colony, Liberia was still heavily dependent on aid from America. But the change in government was proof that the time of white rule in black colonies was passing.

The appointment of another black colonial governor in West Africa strengthened Russwurm's authority and helped him in his dealings with white officials. The boost in prestige came none too soon, because in 1843 he began a battle with the Maryland Society over how much tax the colony should pay

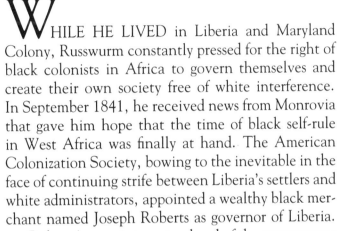

Russwurm's efforts to foster black independence in the West African colonies began to bear fruit during the early 1840s. Shown here is a ceremony to welcome Joseph Roberts, the first black governor of Liberia, upon his return to Monrovia from a trip abroad.

The presence of American slavers on the West African coast upset relations between Maryland Colony and native tribes. In 1839, the revolt of captives on board the slave ship Amistad *focused international attention on the illegal slave trade. Cinque (shown here) led the rebels, who later settled in Sierra Leone.*

on goods imported from America. The conflict arose when the society's directors, seeing the great progress that Maryland Colony was making under its governor's able leadership, imposed a 10 percent tax on all supplies they sent to Cape Palmas. Arguing that the charge was excessive and would impoverish the colony, Russwurm demanded that the tax be lowered to one percent.

The struggle over the tax issue continued until 1846, when the society relented and authorized Russwurm to lower the import charges to whatever rate he believed was fair. This victory was a symbol of the colony's growing independence from its parent organization in America. The small community of former slaves was almost ready to stand on its own.

Exhausted by his demanding schedule, Russwurm nevertheless pushed ahead with his plans to improve the colony. He was especially interested in promoting more advanced agricultural methods. Through his own experimentation, he proved to the settlers that by fertilizing fields and rotating crops (a method of preserving soil productivity by growing crops in different fields each season), they could greatly increase their yields of cassava (a root crop), sweet potatoes, plantains, and other nutritious foods. He also encouraged the farmers to grow cotton and tobacco, money-making trade items for the colony.

Although records of Maryland Colony's affairs still exist, there are few documents remaining that tell about the lives of Russwurm's wife, Sarah, and their children. A personal journal Russwurm kept was either lost or destroyed. But it is known that he and Sarah eventually had five children. Besides their eldest son, George, and James (who died in infancy), the Russwurms had two more sons and one daughter. The older of these two sons was named Frank; the name of their youngest son is unknown. Their only daughter was named Angelina.

As the colony grew, the settlers moved further inland, in search of new land, and they came into closer contact with the local African tribes. Russwurm tried to develop friendly relations with the colony's neighbors by establishing new schools for them, stocking the Africans' favorite trade goods in the colony store, and helping Christian missionaries set up churches on tribal lands. Over the years, marriages and adoptions also helped cement ties between the two peoples.

Despite Russwurm's best efforts, relations between the settlers and Africans had many rocky periods. Disputes over land ownership caused some of the feuds, and the colonists had to be constantly on guard against raids on their supplies. The activities of slave traders were another source of tension. Before the colonists settled in the area, the only Americans that most of the Africans had ever seen were slavers. When ships bearing the American flag arrived at Cape Palmas to deliver supplies, the natives suspected they were slave traders still haunting the West African shores. On several occasions, the colony was nearly attacked by tribes who were seeking loot or revenge for the actions of American slavers.

Russwurm understood the reasons for the Africans' fears about slavers and explained to them that the ships stopping at the colony carried nothing but supplies. He assured the natives that the colonists were violently opposed to slavery, and he told them that he was giving information about slave trading activity to the U.S. warships that patrolled the West African coast in search of slavers. He also explained that the colonists were committed to building a home for themselves in Africa and that they were slowly cutting their ties to America.

Yet Maryland Colony still needed the vital water link to America during the early 1840s. Disease took a heavy toll on the settlers, and the colony's growth

In 1843, Maryland Colony was visited by a U.S. Navy squadron commanded by Commodore Matthew Perry. A foray by a group of Perry's men into tribal territory sparked bloody fighting that jeopardized Russwurm's good relations with native chiefs.

depended on ships bringing a steady flow of immigrants from Maryland. The ships also brought letters
from friends and relatives in America and abolitionist
journals that gave news about the struggle against
slavery. And, as Samuel McGill, the colony's lieu-
tenant governor, noted in a letter, the frequent ap-
pearances of powerful warships at Cape Palmas
showed the native tribes that the colonists were protected by the U.S. Navy.

On at least one occasion, the presence of American warships at Cape Palmas created trouble for
Russwurm. In 1843, a fleet commanded by Commodore Matthew Perry was hunting for slavers on the
African coast when it stopped at the colony to pick
up supplies. The arrival of the ships was especially
welcome to Russwurm because Horatio Bridge, one
of his friends at Bowdoin College, was among Perry's
officers.

Unfortunately, a bloody engagement between
some of Perry's men and a native tribe swept away
Russwurm's initial joy at meeting his old classmate.
While the fleet was at Cape Palmas, a captain of one
of the ships led a group of his sailors on an excursion
into a tribal area. The tribe, perhaps believing that
the naval men were slavers, attacked and killed all
the members of the group. In retaliation, Perry sent
a heavily armed force against the hostile tribe. Three
towns were destroyed and many natives were killed.

Once more, Russwurm was caught in the middle
of a dangerous situation. Although he deplored the
violence on both sides, he realized that the colonists
were dependent on the navy's protection and decided
that he must loyally defend Perry's attack on the
native towns. With the colony's safety in grave jeop-
ardy, he immediately began efforts to restore peace
in the area. Using his good connections with the
local native rulers, he arranged a meeting to discuss
how to bring an end to the fighting. The conference

was attended by Russwurm and a delegation from Maryland Colony, Liberian governor Joseph Roberts, Perry and a group of naval officers, and a powerful native chief named King Freeman.

The peace conference was a huge success for Russwurm, who managed to repair relations with the natives and to bargain for terms that helped safeguard his colony. Negotiating with great skill, he persuaded King Freeman to sell some of his land to the colonists and to move his warriors a greater distance from the colony's borders. Meanwhile, Russwurm also arranged for improved trading relations so that the colonists could sell larger amounts of their surplus farm produce to the natives.

Russwurm had succeeded in turning a potential disaster into a triumph by the time Perry sailed from Cape Palmas shortly after the meeting. As he wrote to Perry at the time of the commodore's departure, "Our prospects have been brighter since the arrival of your squadron on this coast." The colony's position was now much stronger, and Russwurm had little trouble with the native chiefs in his remaining years as governor.

In 1847, Liberia's citizens declared their independence from the American Colonization Society and established the Republic of Liberia. Joseph Roberts, who had been governor of the colony for six years, was elected president.

When peaceful conditions returned to Cape Palmas, Russwurm was able to look with great pride at the progress that his colony was making. The fruits of his efforts to improve the quality of the colonists' lives could be seen in many places. His support for education had helped foster an interest in cultural and intellectual pursuits, one sign of which was the formation of a debating society in 1845. By then, schoolhouses were doing double duty as lecture halls and Sunday schools.

Russwurm's skillful administration of the colony's affairs endeared him to the colonists. On one occasion in the early 1840s, the loyalty of the Cape Palmas settlers to their leader was severely tested. During the worst of the conflicts with the natives, when many people in the colony feared for their lives, a visiting British colonial agent offered to transport the settlers to a South American colony, where life was supposed to be much easier. All the settlers—even the worst of the complainers—decided to stay with their governor. Their support reassured Russwurm that his decision to devote his life to the African colonies had been a wise one.

In 1847, Russwurm and the people of Maryland Colony were excited to learn that Liberia had broken its ties to the American Colonization Society and had formed the Free and Independent Republic of Liberia. Joseph Roberts was elected president of the new nation, and he invited Sarah Russwurm to be one of seven women to design the flag that would fly in Monrovia. They modeled it on the American flag, with a single star on a field of blue. At the same time, Liberia adopted a motto that echoed the hopes of all the colonists who had come to the shores of West Africa: The Love of Liberty Brought Us Here.

The Cape Palmas citizens celebrated with the independent Liberians even though their colony was not part of the new republic. Russwurm had main-

Russwurm's wife, Sarah, was one of the people chosen to create Liberia's flag, whose design and colors were patterned on the American flag.

tained close relations with Monrovia ever since Roberts had become the head of the government there, and he now began working to sever Maryland Colony's ties to America. Yet the colony's final break with the Maryland Society and its merger with Liberia would not occur for another seven years.

Liberia's declaration of independence helped to spur renewed interest in Africa as a home for black Americans. A number of black leaders, including the American physician and editor Martin Delany and the West Indian educator and minister Edward Blyden, urged blacks to open their minds to the idea of emigrating to Liberia or other parts of Africa. Known as the father of African nationalism, Delany organized an exploratory expedition to Africa to search for an area that could be a suitable home for millions of black Americans. Blyden, who settled in Liberia and became editor of the *Liberia Herald*, wrote many books about the history and culture of Africa while attempting to dispel myths that the continent was a land of ignorant savages.

For Russwurm, however, the struggle to build a home in West Africa was reaching an end. He was 50 years old in 1849, and he was ready to take a break from his taxing duties as colonial governor. At about this time, he began to think about returning once again to the home of his youth. Sarah Russwurm had recently sailed on a visit to America with one of their children, and after arranging for Samuel McGill to fill in for him as governor, Russwurm decided to join them.

Russwurm knew this trip would be his last chance to see his American family. Although he had not seen them for 20 years, they had never been far from his thoughts. He was also hoping to take care of his health problems, which had become so severe that any hope for recovery could only come from the more advanced medical treatment available in the United States.

In 1849, Russwurm traveled to the United States and had a last reunion with his stepmother and other family members. While visiting Bowdoin College, he met Senator William Fessenden, who urged him to remain in America and help lead the struggle against slavery.

In 1849, Russwurm made the voyage home that he had dreamed about for so long. He visited Maine and was reunited with his stepmother, Susan Hawes, and the members of his family who still lived there. But he did not see his half brother Francis, who had joined the flood of people who were rushing to California's recently discovered gold-mining fields.

While in Maine, Russwurm arranged for the education of his children. The Cape Palmas school system did not have a high school, and Russwurm was determined that his children be given the opportunity for a higher education. He still saw education as the most powerful weapon for a person, and he resolved that his own children would never be held back by ignorance.

While visiting his own college, Russwurm met William Fessenden, a Bowdoin graduate who served on the college's board of directors. Like Russwurm, Fessenden had been something of an outsider during his college years, and he had been denied his diploma because of his unruly behavior. Undaunted, he had become a successful lawyer and then a member of the U.S. Senate, where he had campaigned for an end to slavery.

Fessenden was greatly impressed by Russwurm's accomplishments at Cape Palmas and tried to persuade him to move back to the United States and join the antislavery movement. Having once been scorned by the abolitionists, Russwurm was pleased that the senator made the request. But he told Fessenden that his home was in Africa with the people who depended on his leadership.

After traveling to Baltimore to meet with officials of the Maryland Society as well as to receive medical treatment, Russwurm sailed back to Africa. The trip to America and the time away from the responsibilities of his office made him feel strong again. Back

The achievements of Russwurm and his fellow colonists inspired many black Americans. Martin Delany, a Harvard-trained physician who led an exploratory expedition to West Africa in 1859, proclaimed, "Africa is our fatherland and we its legitimate descendants. . . . I have outgrown, long since, the boundaries of North America."

at Cape Palmas, he told his friends that his travels had added 12 to 15 years to his life.

Samuel McGill had served so ably as governor of the colony during Russwurm's absence that the returning leader could have reduced his work load and depended more on McGill. Instead, he immediately returned to his routine of working night and day, ignoring the warnings of his family and friends. Within a year, the heavy work load took its toll. He died at Cape Palmas in June 1851, at the age of 52.

The colonists felt the loss of their governor deeply. For 15 years, he had encouraged them to fight for freedom and a better life. He had scratched a living out of the earth alongside them, educating their children and pacifying angry native tribes. He had maintained a supply line to America while at the same time working to create an independent black nation. Most of all, he had shown the colonists that they could turn their backs on the taunts of white racists and build their own proud community.

Russwurm's contributions to the cause of liberty have been recognized in recent times by the establishment of the Russwurm Award, which is presented annually by the National Newspaper Publishers Association to a person who has worked hard to promote democratic ideals.

In grateful memory of
JOHN B. RUSSWURM
first Negro in the United States to receive a college degree, and whose pioneering spirit and clear vision motivated him to establish, in Manhattan in 1827,

FREEDOM'S JOURNAL

the first Negro newspaper and the forerunner of the Negro Press in America, which has conscientiously striven to meet the challenge he initiated.

FREEDOM'S JOURNAL.

After Russwurm's death, Samuel McGill took over officially as governor of Maryland Colony, but the community never regained the sense of direction it had enjoyed under Russwurm's leadership. The colony was finally absorbed into Liberia in 1854. Eleven years later, the United States abolished slavery after a bitter war between the North and the South. The impetus for black emigration to Africa was lost for many years, but the idea was revived by the black nationalist leader Marcus Garvey in the early 1900s. Garvey's "Back to Africa" movement again focused attention on the continent that Russwurm and the founders of Liberia had championed as the home of all the world's black people.

Although Russwurm continued to be honored in Liberia as a founder of the movement for black self-rule in Africa, his name was virtually forgotten in America for more than a century after his death. In more recent times, however, his contributions to the struggle for racial justice have been recognized. Schools and educational scholarships now bear his name, and each year the American Newspaper Publishers Association presents the Russwurm Award for outstanding work in furthering democratic principles. The winners of the award include President John F. Kennedy and the Reverend Martin Luther King, Jr.

A man of firm convictions with the courage to stand up for his beliefs—often against popular opinion—Russwurm devoted his life to showing that a person with vision and determination could not be defeated by racial prejudice. As one of the first black Americans to earn a college degree, as a pioneering journalist and publisher, and as a leader among his people in the West African frontier, he proved his dedication to the principles of liberty and racial equality. The achievements of John Russwurm still stand as an inspiration to all those who dream of building a better world. ☙

Russwurm's gravesite in Cape Palmas

CHRONOLOGY

1799   Born John Brown Russwurm in Port Antonio, Jamaica, on October 1

1807   Moves to Quebec, Canada

1812   Moves to Portland, Maine

1819   Graduates from Hebron Academy; becomes a teacher in Boston, Massachusetts

1826   Graduates from Bowdoin College; moves to New York City

1827   Cofounds *Freedom's Journal*

1829   Announces support for the African colonization movement; resigns from *Freedom's Journal*

1829   Moves to Liberia

1830   Publishes the *Liberia Herald*; becomes colonial secretary

1833   Marries Sarah McGill

1836   Becomes governor of Cape Palmas

1839   Institutes a standard currency system in Maryland Colony

1849   Returns to the United States

1851   Dies at Cape Palmas in June

FURTHER READING

Aptheker, Herbert, ed. *A Documentary History of the Negro People in the United States.* New York: Citadel Press, 1973.

Bennett, Lerone, Jr. *Before the Mayflower.* New York: Penguin, 1984.

——. *Wade in the Water: Great Moments in Black History.* Chicago: Johnson, 1979.

Campbell, Penelope. *Maryland in Africa.* Urbana: University of Illinois Press, 1971.

Dann, Martin E., ed. *The Black Press, 1827–1890.* New York: Capricorn Books, 1971.

Hughes, Langston, and Milton Meltzer. *A Pictorial History of the Negro in America.* New York: Crown, 1956.

Logan, Rayford W., and Michael R. Winston, eds. *Dictionary of American Negro Biography.* New York: Norton, 1982.

Meier, August, and Elliot Rudwick. *From Plantation to Ghetto.* New York: Hill and Wang, 1966.

Sagarin, Mary. *John Brown Russwurm: The Story of Freedom's Journal.* New York: Morrow, 1970.

Shick, Tom W. *Behold the Promised Land: A History of Afro-American Settler Society in Nineteenth-Century Liberia.* Baltimore: Johns Hopkins University Press, 1977.

West, Richard. *Back to Africa.* New York: Holt, Rinehart, and Winston, 1970.

Wiley, Bell I., ed. *Slaves No More: Letters From Liberia, 1833–1869.* Lexington, University of Kentucky Press, 1980.

INDEX

Abolitionists, 25–26, 48, 58, 61–62, 83
African Dorcas Association, 47
African Free Schools, 44, 47
African Methodist Episcopal Church, 25
Allen, Richard, 26, 53
American Colonization Society, 13–14, 50–51, 53, 58–62, 65, 69, 71, 73, 78, 79, 84, 95, 100
Amherst College, 38
Athenaean Society, 35

Back Cove, Maine, 28
"Back to Africa" movement, 105
Baltimore, Maryland, 41
Banneker, Benjamin, 45–46
Blackbirders, 42
Black equality
  black militancy, rise of, 58, 64–65
  free blacks, lives of, 24–25, 31, 41–42, 58, 61
  propaganda of press, 42–43
Blanchard, James (stepbrother), 29
Blanchard, Susanna (step-mother), 28–29, 103
Blyden, Edward, 101
Boston, Massachusetts, 29, 30
Bowdoin College, 31, 33–39, 98, 103
Bridge, Horatio, 35, 98

Cape Palmas, 85–105
Cary, Lott, 69
Christophe, Henri, 20
Clay, Henry, 50
Colonization movement, 13–15, 50–53, 58–65, 76, 79, 84

Colored American, The, 56, 82
Cornish, Samuel, 42, 44, 46–50, 53, 55–56, 82
Cuffe, Paul, 45

Dailey, Joseph, 75–76
Delany, Martin, 101
Dessalines, Jean-Jacques, 20

Eastern Argus, 38

Fessenden, William, 98, 103
Finley, Robert, 50
Five Corners, New York City, 41
Force, Charles, 72–73
Forten, James, 26, 53
Free African Society, 25
Freedom Day, 48
Freedom's Journal, 11, 12, 15
  on black women, 47–48
  on colonization movement, 50, 51, 53, 62–65
  Cornish resigns, 55–57
  Cornish-Russwurm partner-ship, 44, 46–50, 53, 55–56
  distribution of, 48–49
  financial difficulties, 49
  founding of, 44
  goals of, 45, 50
  Paul Cuffe feature, 45
  Russwurm resigns, 65
  on slavery issue, 46, 49–50
  types of articles in, 46

Garrison, William Lloyd, 14, 82
Garvey, Marcus, 105
Grain Coast, 68
Great Britain, 83

Haiti, 20, 37, 39

Hall, James, 85, 87
Hall, Primus, 29
Harper settlement, 88, 89, 90–91
Hawes, William, 29
Hawthorne, Nathaniel, 33, 35
Hebron Academy, 29
Horton, Gilbert, 46

Jackson, Andrew, 27
Jamaica, 17, 20
Jefferson, Thomas, 50
Jones, Absalom, 26
Jones, Edward, 38

King Freeman, 99

Latrobe, John, 86, 89
Liberator, The, 15, 82
Liberia, 51, 59, 62, 65, 67–79, 83–84, 95, 100, 105
Liberia Herald, 72, 73, 75, 77, 79, 101
Longfellow, Henry Wadsworth, 33
L'Ouverture, Toussaint, 20

McGill, George, 72, 75
McGill, Samuel, 90, 98, 104, 105
McGill, Sarah. See Russwurm, Sarah
Madison, James, 50
Maroons, 19
Maryland Colony, 85–105
Maryland Society, 84–85, 86, 87, 89, 90, 92, 93, 95
"Matilda," 48
Mechlin, Joseph, 72, 73, 75, 76
Missouri Compromise, 30–31
Monroe, James, 51
Monrovia, Liberia, 51, 67, 68,

70, 72, 76, 82, 85, 95,
100–101

Negro Presbyterian Church, 44
New Orleans, Battle of, 27–28
New York, 39, 41
Noah, Mordecai, 43

Perry, Matthew, 98–99
Pierce, Franklin, 33
Pinney, John, 76–78
Portland, Maine, 22, 26
Prince Hall Freemasons, 25
Prosser, Gabriel, 26
Prout, Jacob, 76

Quebec, Canada, 20–21

*Remonstrance Against the Abuse
of Blacks, A* (Cornish), 42
Rights of All, The, 65
Roberts, Joseph, 95, 99, 100
Russwurm, Angelina (daugh-
ter), 96
Russwurm, Francis Edward
(brother), 29, 76, 79, 103
Russwurm, Frank (son), 96
Russwurm, George (son), 75,
96
Russwurm, James (son), 87, 96
Russwurm, John Brown

as abolitionist, 39, 58
agricultural projects, 89, 96
blacks turn against, 11–15,
64–65, 77–78
colonization movement and,
13–15, 53, 58–65, 76, 79,
84
death of, 104
early years, 17–23, 29
education, 20, 22, 29, 31,
33–39, 65
final trip to America, 102–3
as governor of Maryland Colony, 87–105
Haiti, interest in, 36–37, 39
in Liberia, 15, 67–79, 83–84
and *Liberia Herald,* 72, 73,
75, 77, 79
marriage, 75, 96
relations with African tribes,
91–92, 97, 99, 100
school system, founding of,
90, 92
speaks at college graduation,
38–39
standard currency, establishment of, 92–93
as teacher, 29
in trading business, 75
See also Freedom's Journal.
Russwurm, John, Sr. (father),

17, 20, 21, 23
Russwurm, Sarah (wife), 75,
79, 96, 100, 102
Russwurm Award, 105

Sierra Leone, 68
Skinner, Ezekiel, 78, 79
Slave Coast, 68
Slavery
in America, 18–19, 25, 30–
31
Missouri Compromise and,
30–31
Turner's uprising, 82–83
in West Indies, 19–20
Smyth, William, 36
Stowe, Harriet Beecher, 33

Teage, Hiliary, 76
Turner, Nat, 82–83, 84

Uncle Tom's Cabin (Stowe), 33
Underground Railroad, 21, 36
Upham, Thomas, 36

Walker, David, 64
Walker's Appeal, 64
War of 1812, 26–27
West Indies, 19–20
Wheatley, Phillis, 45
Williams, Peter, 26, 42

PICTURE CREDITS

JANICE BORZENDOWSKI holds a degree in journalism and Russian from the University of Arizona. She has written for *Advertising Age* and has worked for several publishers in New York City, including Harcourt Brace Jovanovich. She has also been manager of publications for New York University's Graduate School of Business. She is currently director of publications for the American Society for the Prevention of Cruelty to Animals (ASPCA).

NATHAN IRVIN HUGGINS is W.E.B. Du Bois Professor of History and Director of the W.E.B. Du Bois Institute for Afro-American Research at Harvard University. He previously taught at Columbia University. Professor Huggins is the author of numerous books, including *Black Odyssey: The Afro-American Ordeal in Slavery, The Harlem Renaissance,* and *Slave and Citizen: The Life of Frederick Douglass.*

MLib